WHY NEO

Post industrial society seems to be polarized between cultural nihilism for the intellectuals and self-delusion, credulity and superstition for the masses. For millions of intelligent and educated people, the ancient human urge toward transcendence can no longer be satisfied though faith in the dying religions of the father. In the age of science, belief and faith have become irrelevant; it is precisely this that makes neo-shamanism increasingly important. Shamanism discards belief or faith. It suggests that you trust your own visionary experiences. It offers ancient techniques that produce immediate results. It suggests that you retain only what works to enhance your personal growth, freedom, and autonomy, and that you discard the rest.

The techniques described in this book will teach you how to tap sources of inner wisdom and raise power. Gradually and properly used, this power enables you to generate positive synchronicities that can alter so-called "chance" life events and thus enhance personal satisfaction, harmony, integration and wholeness. Use of the techniques will also increase your ability to control various aspects of your life. Shamanic practice releases beta-endorphins and produces euphoria. This makes it an effective antidote against feelings of depression.

This book is written for non-credulous people who believe in facing up to the unpleasant aspects of reality. Gnosis means knowledge, and in the late 20th century all genuine knowledge must be sifted from self-delusion and superstition by a relentless demand for empirical results and pragmatic effectiveness. Here, the esoteric tradition is subjected to friendly but critical scrutiny. We show you how you can be a powerful occultist or ritual magician, and at the same time retain your intelligent skepticism and critical mind.

About the Authors

ANGELIQUE S. COOK maintains a private practice in Albuquerque, New Mexico, as an Acupuncture physician and shaman. She has been a clairvoyant since childhood. Over the past two decades, Angelique has consulted for individuals and corporations.

G.A. HAWK is the pen name of George A. Huaco, Ph.D., an academic, who teaches at a university in the southwest. In addition, he teaches private workshops on neoshamanism.

To Write to the Authors

We cannot guarantee that every letter written to the authors can be answered, but all will be forwarded. Both the authors and the publisher appreciate hearing from readers, learning of your enjoyment and benefit from this book. Llewellyn also publishes a bimonthly news magazine with news and reviews of practical esoteric studies and articles helpful to the student. Some readers' questions and comments to the authors may be answered through this magazine's columns if permission to do so is included in the original letter. The authors sometimes participate in seminars and workshops, and dates and places are announced in *The Llewellyn New Times*. To write to the authors, or to ask a question, write to:

Angelique S. Cook and G. A. Hawk
c/o THE LLEWELLYN NEW TIMES
P.O. Box 643483-325, St. Paul, MN 55164-0383, U.S.A.

Please enclose a self-addressed, stamped envelope for reply, or $1.00 to cover costs.

SHAMANISM AND THE ESOTERIC TRADITION

Angelique S. Cook and G. A. Hawk

1992
Llewellyn Publications
St. Paul, Minnesota 55164-0383 U.S.A.

FIRST EDITION

Library of Congress Cataloging-in-Publication Data
Cook, Angelique S.
 Shamanism and the esoteric tradition / by Angelique S. Cook and
G.A. Hawk.
  p. cm. — (Llewellyn's new worlds spirituality series)
 Includes bibliographical references
 ISBN 0-97542-325-6
 1. Shamanism. 2. Occultism. I. Hawk, G.A. (George A.)
II. Title. III. Series
BF1611.C725 1992
133.4'3—dc20   92-5607
                                                    CIP

Llewellyn Publications
A Division of Llewellyn Worldwide, Ltd.
P.O. Box 64383, St. Paul, MN 55164-0383

Spirituality may be best defined as the attainment of the highest aspects of human character in relationship to the Divine. In the past, this attainment was most often under the control of fixed doctrines and hierarchical religious structures. Today, however, this quest for spirituality has become more of an individual process. Spirituality has become a process of making a personal connection to the highest, most divine aspects of Self.

One of the strongest concepts, basic to the quest for spirituality in modern times, is the deep recognition of the unity and interrelatedness of all aspects of life. While this concept may have been given lip service in the past, it is being practiced in the present. We are indeed living in a new world of awareness, consciousness, and connectedness.

Ancient wisdom, which predates the teachings of most organized religions, speaks of this same great unity of life. Often this is described as a web, or weaving, of which we are all an active, creative part. Even modern physics has come full circle to meet ancient mysticism with its "new physics" concept of a tissue of events connecting all life. Spirituality has become the domain of each individual in full awareness of his role, and his function in the weaving of life.

As we, too, have come full circle, we have begun to view ancient wisdoms and forms of spirituality with new, and renewed, interest. Many of these ancient spiritual forms carry the message of direct connection to the Divine that we seek today. Moreover, they connect us directly to the web of life by reacquainting us with Nature, with Spirit, and with our most personal, divine Self. Rather than doctrine, these ancient spiritual forms provide direction; rather than dogma, they give us decisive power in our own lives.

In a new world of spirituality, we turn back to ancient forms such as shamanism, Wicca and earth wisdoms to reclaim sovereignty over our own spiritual lives. We relearn ancient ways so that we can follow our own path and make a direct connection to the most divine aspects of Self, Nature, and Spirit. Our path, we see now, is one active thread in the great weaving of life we call the universe. And our renewed awareness of our function as part of this weaving show us that we are both the weaving and the weaver. In the new world we share, we find that the quest for spirituality is a personal responsibility—one with positive power and with results to be shared by all.

ACKNOWLEDGMENTS

Grateful acknowledgment is made for permission to use excerpts from copyrighted material as follows:

From pp. 347, 450, 508-509 of Mircea Eliade. 1964. *Shamanism : Archaic Techniques of Ecstasy*. Princeton, NJ: Princeton University Press. Copyright © 1964 by Bollingen Foundation. Reprinted by permission of Princeton University Press.

From p. 102 of Frances A. Yates. 1969. *Giordano Bruno and the Hermetic Tradition*. New York: Vintage. Copyright © 1964 by Frances A. Yates. Reprinted by permission of the University of Chicago Press.

From pp. 111,112,114 of Gershom G. Scholem. 1969. *On the Kabbalah and Its Symbolism*. New York, NY: Schocken. English translation copyright © by Schocken Books, Inc. Reprinted by permission of Random House, Inc.

From p. 203 of Francis King. 1970. *The Rites of Modern Occult Magic*. New York: Macmillan. Copyright © 1970 by Francis King. Reprinted by permission of Georges Borchardt, Inc.

From p. 86 of J. H. Brennan. 1971. *Astral Doorways*. York Beach, ME: Samuel Weiser, Inc. and London: Aquarian Press UK, a division of Harper Collins. Copyright © 1971 by J. H. Brennan. Reprinted by permission of Samuel Weiser, Inc.

From p. 237 of Gershom G. Scholem. 1972. *Major Trends in Jewish Mysticism*. New York, NY: Schocken. Copyright © 1941, 1946, 1954, 1961 by Schocken Publishing House. Reprinted by permission of Random House, Inc.

From pp. 76, 184 of Marie-Louise Von Franz. 1974. *Shadow and Evil In Fairytales*. Zurich: Spring Publications. Copyright © 1974 by Marie-Louise Von Franz. Reprinted by permission of Marie-Louise Von Franz and of Shambhala Publications, Inc.

From p. 281 of Joseph Campbell. 1976. *Masks of God : Primitive Mythology*. New York: Penguin. Copyright © 1959, 1969, renewed 1987 by Joseph Campbell. Reprinted by permission of Viking Penguin, a division of Penguin Books USA, Inc.

From p. 60 of Aryeh Kaplan. 1979. *The Bahir*. York Beach, ME: Samuel Weiser, Inc. Copyright © 1979 Aryeh Kaplan. Reprinted by permission of Samuel Weiser, Inc.

From p. 119 of Melita Denning and Osborne Phillips. 1980. *Psychic Self-Defense and Well-Being*. St. Paul, MN: Llewellyn Publications. Copyright © 1980 by Melita Denning and Osborne Phillips. Reprinted by permission of Llewellyn Publications.

From pp. 27–28 of V. N. Basilov. 1984. "Chosen by the Spirits," pp. 3–48 in Marjorie Mandelstam Balzer ed. and trans. 1990. *Shamanism : Soviet Studies of Traditional Religion in Siberia and Central Asia*. Armonk, NY: M. E. Sharpe, Inc. Copyright © 1990 by M. E. Sharpe, Inc. Reprinted by .permission of Basil Blackwell Publishers, Oxford UK.

From p. 7 of Peter J. Carroll. 1987. *Liber Null and Psychonaut*. York Beach, ME: Samuel Weiser, Inc. Copyright © 1987 by Peter J. Carroll. Reprinted by permission of Samuel Weiser, Inc.

From p. 105 of Jonn Mumford. 1988. *Ecstasy Through Tantra*. St. Paul, MN: Llewellyn Publications. Copyright © 1975, 1977, 1987 by Jonn Mumford. Reprinted by permission of Llewellyn Publications.

From pp. 104, 124–125 of Doreen Valiente. 1989. *The Rebirth of Witchcraft*. London: Robert Hale, Ltd. Copyright © 1989 by Doreen Valiente. Reprinted by permission of Robert Hale, Ltd.

From pp. 337 and 341 of T. M. Luhrmann. 1989. *Persuasions of the Witch's Craft : Ritual Magic in Contemporary England*. Cambridge, MA: Harvard University Press. Copyright © 1989 by T.M. Luhrmann. Reprinted by permission of Harvard University Press.

In addition, we wish to thank our friends Llew Wykel and Karol Kelly who designed the graphics.

CONTENTS

INTRODUCTION

The purpose of this work is to explore the relations between ancient shamanism and contemporary occultism as exemplified in the activities of ritual magicians and Witches in urban-industrial society. We have written from the point of view of insiders and practitioners, which means that this is not an exercise in skeptical rationalism or a scientific ethnography. Our focus is on techniques that produce results. It is our hope that this enterprise will show neo-shamans that their practice can be enhanced by the incorporation of some esoteric techniques developed in the last 6,000 years. Likewise, it is our hope that this work will show practitioners of Witchcraft and ritual magic that they can enhance and revitalize their practice by returning to, and borrowing from, their ancient source: the shamanism of the hunters and gatherers.

Amid the pervasive nihilism of the late 20th century, the ancient human urge to transcend the human condition has lost none of its urgency. But more often than not, that urge operates in a context of disorientation and bewilderment, surrounded by dying religions and the commercialism of new age superstition. As an alternative to all of this, we offer neo-shamanism and a critical version of the esoteric tradition. Shamanism is not a religion, as the term religion is understood in the West. Religion emphasizes *belief* in a set of doctrines about the supernatural. Shamanism emphasizes visionary *experience*, and holds belief to be irrelevant or unimportant.

Superstition has been defined as false beliefs about causal relationships which result in unnecessary and ineffective behavior (Walsh, 1990: 37). There is no question but that shamanism in its tribal setting, and Witchcraft and ritual magic in their historical contexts, are loaded down with much superstition. To identify and reject culturally relative tribal taboos is fairly easy. A much more difficult task is to try and separate ineffective behavior from effective techniques in areas such as ritual magic or the paranormal, which do not lend themselves to controlled experimentation. As a minimum, we need a total rejection of credulity and a critical demand that any and all procedures justify themselves in terms of results.

These pragmatic tests are not an innovation of our scientific civilization. Soviet ethnologist B. N. Basilov describes how various tribes of Siberia and Central Asia (the Nganasan, the Khanty, the Ket, the Kazakh, the Ul'chi, and the Nanai) tested their shamans for psychic vision and precognitive abilities. For example, while wearing a blindfold the shaman had to accomplish certain tasks such as finding various objects, walking on the tundra without falling into holes or bumping into rocks, stepping over a trip rope which had been placed on the ground or licking red-hot metal while remaining unharmed. Among the Ul'chi and the Nanai, the shaman had to prove that he was seeing the spirits of the dead by giving a correct description of the circumstances surrounding the death of each person.

Testing of the shaman took different forms among the varied peoples, but its meaning was always the same: the

shaman had to demonstrate in practice that the spirits were rendering him aid. The authority of the shaman...depended on successful healing, predictions coming true, accurate counsel.
Basilov, 1984: 27-28

In a recent work, Roger N. Walsh has successfully specified five definitional characteristics of shamanism. A shaman is:

a. Someone who enters and leaves altered states of consciousness at will.

b. While in these altered states of consciousness, this person experiences journeying to various domains of the inner world.

c. This journeying is done to obtain power and knowledge, and to help other people.

d. While on these journeys, this person enters a transcendent reality which is usually hidden from the rest of humanity.

e. While in an altered state of consciousness, this person interacts with power animals, teachers, demonic intrusions, and the spirits of the dead.

As Walsh correctly points out, the first three characteristics are purely empirical, while the fourth and fifth seem to involve philosophical and religious assumptions (Walsh, 1990: 10-11).

Alternatively, what do we mean when we say that a shaman interacts with spirits? Are we claiming that spirits exist? As the contemporary German magician Frater U.'. D.'. has pointed out, the answer depends on the language and the model which you use to interpret your visionary experience (Frater U.'. D.'. , 1990: 5). In the traditional spirit model, spirits most definitely do exist. If we use the energy model, then we talk about forms of energy. If we use the information model, then we talk about information clusters. If we use the Jungian psychological model, then we talk about semi-autonomous complexes and archetypes of the collective unconscious. But an archetype, which is a form of energy and a cluster of information, seems indistinguishable from what traditionalists mean by a spirit.

Walsh's list can be used to make a preliminary distinction between shamanism and other states, callings, and conditions. Priests do not enter altered states of consciousness and do not journey. Mediums enter altered states of consciousness at will and interact with spirits; but they do not journey, and their interaction with spirits is likely to take the form of possession. Those suffering from mental illness enter altered states of consciousness and interact with "spirits," but as involuntary victims. Meditators enter altered states of consciousness at will, but do not journey. Finally, medicine men do not journey (Walsh, 1990: 12). The only people who do exactly what shamans do are contemporary occultists, namely ritual magicians, sorcerers, Witches and neo-shamans. And this suggests that occultism is the survival of shamanism in the urban industrial world of the late twentieth century. But shamanism, either as neo-shamanism or as Witchcraft and ritual magic, is not just a survival, it may well belong to the future. As the late Joseph Campbell wrote,

> The binding of the shamans [i.e., the Titans] ... by the gods and their priests, which commenced with the victory of the neolithic over the paleolithic way of life, may perhaps be already terminating—today—in this period of the irreversible transition of society from an agricultural to an industrial base, when not the piety of the planter, bowing humbly before the will of the calendar and the gods of rain and sun, but the magic of the laboratory, flying rocketships where gods once sat, holds the promise of the booms of the future.
>
> Campbell, 1976: 281

Why is shamanism valuable for people in urban-industrial society? More specifically, what has it done for us?

Angelique: I was born with certain psychic abilities; in particular, clairvoyance or the ability to foretell the future, and psychic vision. At age eight, I was lucid dreaming and engaging in astral projection. From my late teens, my guides taught me how to help the spirits of the dead, how to create a balance in a person by doing an exorcism or the removal of parasitic intrusions, and how to bring back a person's missing parts. This leaves a person whole and able to experience life from a balanced state.

In the early 1980s, I read Michael Harner's book, *The Way of the Shaman,* and discovered how to meet my power animal and tap the energy of the Lower World. It is a well-known fact that the practice of psychic abilities tends to unbalance the physical organism. Some mediums become obese, others tend to develop nervous disorders. In my case, the lack of balance manifested as a history of chronic illnesses. The more I engaged in ritual magic, Tarot readings, and psychic work, the less physical energy I had at my disposal. Then I discovered that shamanic journeys with a power animal increased my physical energy and restored the missing equilibrium.

In the mid-1980s, I met a gifted shaman, Sandra Ingerman, of the Foundation for Shamanic Studies. By attending her workshops, I was able to further explore various levels of the Lower World. This has improved my health, and the practice of shamanism has enhanced my healing skills.

George: I have no psychic abilities, but do have a certain facility for eliciting the phenomena of ritual magic. I have been studying the occult or esoteric traditions of both East and West for many years. In the

mid-1980s I discovered shamanism thanks to Michael
Harner and Sandra Ingerman. Since then, intensive
year-round practice has led me to modify some of
their procedures. I have discovered how to use shamanism to experience the birth trauma, and how to
use shamanism for a controlled and completely safe
form of past-life regression. In the use of mantic methods such as the *I Ching,* the shamanic trance makes the
difference between obtaining only mediocre proba-
bilistic results and obtaining significant synchronicities. The shamanic trance dramatically enhances a
modern practice such as sigil magic. Every occult or
esoteric ritual and practice is enhanced and empow-
ered by being reconnected to shamanism or recast in a
shamanic framework. In addition, shamanic practice
produces euphoria and this is an effective antidote
against depression. Shamanism provides you with an
enormously powerful set of techniques that can be
used for self-healing, personal growth, and enhanced
control over the circumstances that affect your life.

PRELIMINARY PRACTICE

Although you will get good results from shamanic
techniques without any prior training, complete success with
some of the other exercises requires a measure of mental discipline or the ability to reach a conscious state of no-thought,
or as the Hindus say, to quiet the chatter of the mind. There
are numerous Eastern exercises for improving your skills in
this direction. Buddhist meditation in which you sit quietly
and concentrate on the breath will do it. Zen meditation will
do it. Hindu exercises in which you deliberately and gradually slow down the breath (while taking deeper breaths) will
do it. You can also lie down, relax, concentrate on becoming
absolutely motionless for about five minutes, and then concentrate on lengthening the empty spaces between thoughts.

We recommend the following exercise which makes use of the shamanic trance:

1. Sit in a comfortable meditation posture. Some people will try a lotus or a half lotus. We recommend kneeling on a foam rubber pad, and sitting on a Japanese *Seiza* bench (This is a small bench in which the seat slants forward).

2. Sit facing a full-length mirror and relax.

3. Use a source of monotonous sonic input (e.g., a drumming tape or the John Stannard Energy Chime) to enter the shamanic trance. If you use the Energy Chime, place it on the rubber pad, and strike it with one hand.

4. Stare at yourself in the mirror with your eyes out of focus (i.e., try to look at the entire mirror at the same time).

5. Inwardly, focus your consciousness on your sense of self, wherever it be located (inside the chest, throat, or head).

6. Empty your mind. Every time you catch yourself drifting into thoughts, stop, and return to conscious no-thought.

7. Do this for about 15 minutes (you can use a timer). The best time is in the morning, before breakfast. We also recommend a partially darkened room.

You may want to read ahead to the explanations given in the next few chapters, and then return to this exercise.

CHAPTER ONE

SHAMANISM AND THE OCCULT

Shamanism is the quest for vision-
ary experience. Humans seek visionary experience because it
is euphoric and can be used for healing, because it gives
access to needed knowledge or wisdom and because it offers
the opportunity to increase control over external circumstances. The quest for healing focuses on the psychic side of
the psychosomatic phenomenon and gives rise to the techniques of restoring vital energy and removing noxious spiritual intrusions. The quest for knowledge or wisdom that is
unobtainable by ordinary means gives rise to techniques of
divination and the search for paranormal abilities such as
clairvoyance and other forms of extrasensory perception. The
quest for increased control over the external circumstances of
one's life leads to the development of ritual magic. Thus shamanism is the source of the entire esoteric tradition in both
East and West.

Shamanism was the spiritual technology of the age of
the hunters. Today we observe a correlation between shamanism and hunting and gathering societies, and its virtual dis-

appearance in agricultural societies (Walsh, 1990: 15). This suggests that shamanism flourished during the Paleolithic period, the half-million years of the age of the great hunt. With the spread of agriculture (from about 11,000 B.C.E.) and the rise of the first governments, the individualistic spiritual technology of shamanism was displaced by religions based on faith and administered by a priesthood. In each case, the doctrines of a visionary founder were recast into dogma and imposed on a docile population by indoctrination, persuasion, fear and coercion. The religions of faith fit in with the needs of governments which organize and control populations. Shamanism does not fit because its ethos is spiritual anarchism. Though persecuted, shamanic activity survived within historical societies, as did yoga and tantra in the East, and as occultism, Witchcraft, and ritual magic did in the West. It also survived in something close to its original form in the tribal cultures of the three southern subcontinents: in the Amazonian rain forest of South America, in Africa south of the Sahara and in aboriginal Australia.

A review of the massive compilations of world-wide shamanic practices (Eliade, 1964; Campbell, 1986), reveals that what Michael Harner calls *core shamanism* (Harner, 1980), is cross-culturally identical. The shaman shifts into an altered state of consciousness in order to journey in non-ordinary reality. The journey produces feelings of euphoria or what Eliade calls "ecstasy." In this journey the shaman is accompanied by his/her power animal, ally, guide, or familiar. The journey is into a domain which later occultists call the "inner planes" and which Carl Jung called the "collective unconscious."

The purpose of the journey may be to promote healing: by retrieving portions of someone's vital essence, by bringing them an ally or by extracting parasitical intrusions lodged in the etheric body. Alternatively, the purpose of the journey may be to obtain desperately needed knowledge about a future outcome or wisdom and advice on how to live. Some shamans act as *psychopomps*, and journey to help the dead move on to their proper region of the inner planes.

Other shamans journey to bring game for the hunters, avert a threat to the community, or to change a noxious external condition. The assumption that in an altered state of consciousness an inner plane subjective operation can change an objective external state of affairs may be completely irrational, but it is justified pragmatically: it works.

Crucial to shamanic activity is the technology for control and safe entry into an altered state of consciousness. Anthropologists and ethnobotanists tell us that on a world-wide basis, entry into shamanic consciousness is done in one of two ways. Some cultures use hallucinogens. Here effectiveness is enhanced at the cost of loss of control and sometimes toxic side-effects. Furthermore, hallucinogens are not equally available all over the planet: the Americas have over 30 sources, while all of Eurasia has seven or eight. Some cultures enter shamanic consciousness by the use of monotonous sonic input (drums, rattles) and dancing. This procedure is completely safe, offers a maximum of control and is extraordinarily effective. Part of its effectiveness may well be due to the fact that the human fetus listens to many months of drumming sounds (produced by the mother's heartbeat and arteries).

The basic schema of the shamanic inner world may be described as follows. In the center of the world is a circle divided into 4 cardinal points. These points are guarded by culturally-specific symbols: power animals, the four children of Horus, the four Christian evangelists, the four meditation Buddhas, the four Elemental Kings of ritual magic. In the center of this circle rises the World Tree or the World Mountain: *Yggdrasil*, the Tree of Life of the Garden of Eden, the Tree of the Kabbalah, or the Sumerian Ziggurat, the Egyptian pyramid, mount Meru of Buddhism or mount Sinai. This tree or mountain gives the shaman access to the three basic regions or domains: the Lower World, the Middle World, and the Upper World. The Lower World contains the power animals, allies, or familiars. The Middle World contains confused, trapped, or destructive spirits, and some dead humans. The Middle World also contains the records of past lives and intimations of the future. The Upper World contains guides or teachers in human form, and what some cultures call gods and goddesses.

THE ELEMENTS

Six thousand years of human history and occult investigations have added some important and original innovations to the legacy of prehistoric shamanism. Among these, the theory of the elements is a cornerstone of further developments. Actually, there are two sets of elements:

The Chinese Elements:
Fire, Metal, Wood/Wind, Water, and Earth.

The Tantric Hindu-Buddhist Elements:
Earth, Water, Fire, Air, and Akasha/Aether.

Thanks in part to classical Greece, the esoteric tradition of western Europe adopted the Tantric-Hindu-Buddhist elements. They are as follows:

Earth : The inert, motionless, solid, rigid, stable, heavy. It is associated with smell.

Water : Condensation, contraction, shrinkage, cohesion. It is associated with taste.

Fire : Expansion, explosion. It is associated with sight.

Air : Weightless, flexible movement. It is associated with touch.

Akasha/
Aether : The "stuff" of the etheric/astral inner planes. It is associated with sound.

Ophiel, 1972: 19-54; Woodroffe, 1981: 19;
Guenther, 1978: 56

Money, material possessions, sexual pleasure, food and drink are Earth. Love, friendship, nurturing are cohesion, and therefore Water. Anger, will, aggression, and leadership are Fire. Intellect and mental operations are Air. Earth and Air (body and mind) are opposites. Water and Fire (love and aggression) are opposites. They are also the Freudian libido and the Jungian archetypal pair of Anima and Animus. The fifth element, which the Hindus call Akasha, and European occultists call Aether or Spirit, is the source of the other four elements, and outside ordinary space-time reality.

These elements are associated with the cardinal points and arranged around the circle in two fundamentally different ways. The very popular sequential, counter-clockwise arrangement is traceable to Jewish "Chariot" or *Merkabah* mysticism of c. 538 B.C.E., and within that, to the vision of Ezekiel:

> *...and there in the heart of it, in the very heart of the fire, was a glow like amber, that enclosed four living figures. These were human in appearance but each had four faces and two pairs of wings ... As for the appearance of their faces, each had the face of a man, yet each of the four looked like a lion when seen from the right, like an ox when seen from the left, like an eagle when seen from above.*
>
> *Ezekiel I, 4 ff*

This can be diagramed as shown in figure one.

The arrangement of Ezekiel describes a pattern in which three animals and one human guard the four cardinal points. A remote ancestor of this pattern is found in the Egyptian Pyramid Texts, c. 2494-2394 B.C.E. (Lurker, 1980: 66, 132). Horus, the divine falcon, the son of Isis and Osiris, had four sons. Three have animal heads (falcon, ape, jackal), and the fourth has a human head. The Four Sons of Horus became the *canopic jars*. Canopic jars were containers found in burial

EAGLE
(above)

OX
(left)

LION
(right)

MAN
(below)

—*Figure One*—
The sequential order of the elements
according to Ezekiel.

chambers with the mummys. By the New Empire, c. 1567-1085 B.C.E., they had become identified as guardians of the four cardinal points (Lurker, 1980: 37-38, 133). See figure two.

**JACKAL
(Duamutef)**

**APE
(Hapi)**

**MAN
(Imsety)**

E

N ← → S

W

**FALCON
(Qebsenneuf)**

—Figure Two—
The canopic jars, their animal symbolism,
and the four directions.

As far as we know, the ancient Egyptians were not familiar with the doctrine of the elements. However, the arrangement of Ezekiel can be interpreted in terms of elements. Since the Ox has to be Earth, and the Lion has to be Fire, and the Eagle has to be Air, it follows that the Man has to be Water. See figure three.

AIR
(Eagle)

EARTH   **FIRE**
(Ox)   **(Lion)**

WATER
(Man)

—*Figure Three*—
The elements and their
symbolic animals.

Here we have the symbols of the four Christian evangelists. In Christian iconography, John is represented by an eagle, Mark by a lion, Matthew by a man and Luke by an ox. We also have the original version of the Earth-Water-Fire-Air sequential, counterclockwise arrangement that is in widespread use among contemporary covens and lodges of ritual magic.

The competitor of the sequential, counterclockwise arrangement is the *polar arrangement* of the elements on the cardinal points. The shaman or magician stands in the center, between the polar opposites. Let us examine this arrangement in Mahayana Tantric Buddhism. The five *Tathagatas* or meditation Buddhas were introduced about 750 C.E. (Conze, 1975: 146, 189). See figure four.

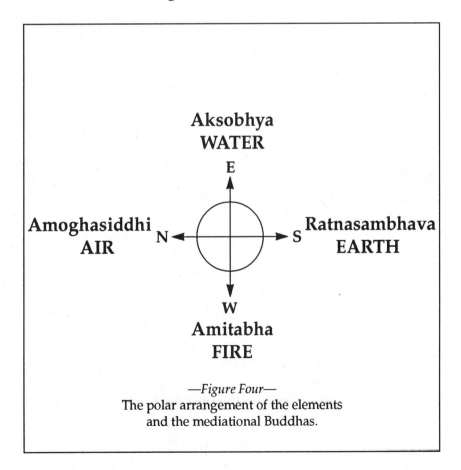

—Figure Four—
The polar arrangement of the elements
and the mediational Buddhas.

This is a polar arrangement: Earth opposes Air and Water opposes Fire. The fifth Buddha, Vairocana, is associated with Akasha and rules the center. Here we find an East-West Fire-Water inversion, traces of which can be found in the symbolism and iconography. Amitabha is red, which is proper for Fire, but his throne sits on a *Padma* or lotus, associated with Water. Aksobhya is blue, which is proper for Water, but he holds a *Vajra* or thunderbolt associated with Fire. No such transposition is found in the iconography of the other two Buddhas. Ratnasambhava is gold-yellow and the lord of jewels which is proper for Earth. Amoghasiddhi is green and sits on a bird-man throne which is proper for Air (Govinda, 1982: 108–110, 114, 121–122; Snellgrove, 1959: 129; Lauf, 1977: 63–73).

Further evidence for an East-West mirror inversion of Fire and Water can be found when we examine the psychological characteristics associated with the Tathagatas. Ratnasambhava is associated with wealth, and that belongs to Earth. Amoghasiddhi is associated with reality-testing, and that belongs to Air. But Amitabha in the West, the red lord of Fire, is associated with love, friendship, compassion, mothering, and sexuality as beauty, all of which belong to the element Water. And Aksobhya in the East, the blue lord of Water, is associated with firmness, courage, bravery, heroism, all of which belong to the element Fire (Trungpa, 1981: 78–84).

The removal of the East-West mirror inversion of Fire and Water can be seen when we examine the negative aspects of the Tathagatas as *Herukas.* See figure five.

Ratna Heruka in the South is associated with greed, avarice, and ostentation (or the element Earth). Karma Heruka in the North is associated with envy, rationalization, and rejection of reality-testing (or the element Air). Padma Heruka in the West is associated with sexuality as possessiveness and bondage (or the element Water). Vajra Heruka in the East is associated with hate, revenge, anger, and aggression (or the element Fire) (Snellgrove, 1959: 93; Trungpa, 1981: 79–80, 83–84, 104–105; Govinda, 1982: 205, 208).

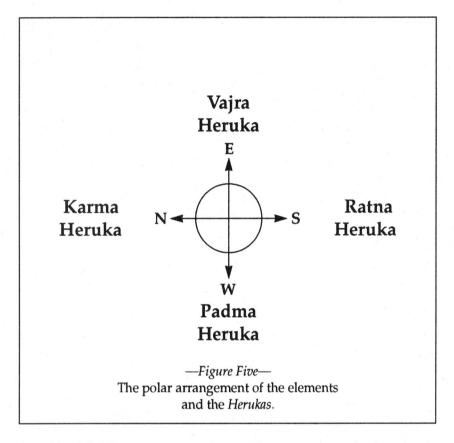

**Vajra
Heruka**

**Karma
Heruka**

**Ratna
Heruka**

**Padma
Heruka**

—*Figure Five*—
The polar arrangement of the elements
and the *Herukas*.

The Christian Gospels say that Jesus taught his disciples a particular prayer, the "Our Father." If we assume that
Fire is in the East, this famous prayer follows a clockwise sequence around a polar arrangement. "Our Father who art in
Heaven, Hallowed be Thy Name": let us assume that these
opening lines identify with the fifth element or Spirit. "Thy
kingdom come. Thy *will* be done. On earth as it is in Heaven."
Here the terms "kingdom" (or power) and "will" identify with
the element Fire. "Give us this day our daily *bread*." "Bread"
identifies with the element Earth. "And *forgive* us our debts as
we *forgive* our debtors." "Forgiveness identifies with the element Water. "Lead us not into temptation but deliver us from
evil." As will be explained below, "evil" identifies with the
North, and therefore with the element Air. See figure six.

One of the key texts of the Kabbalah, the book *Bahir* (c. 1170 C.E.), quotes Jeremiah 1:14 "From the north will evil come forth, upon all the inhabitants of the earth." The text of the *Bahir* goes on to say that "Any evil that comes to 'all the in-habitants of the earth' comes from the north." (*Bahir*, 1170: 60, para. 162). This suggests that Jesus was familiar with the quotation from Jeremiah, and possibly with some of the Jewish Gnostic esotericism which eventually produced the Kabbalah.

In the 1960s, retired Cambridge archeologist and psychic investigator Tom C. Lethbridge, discovered that the dowsing

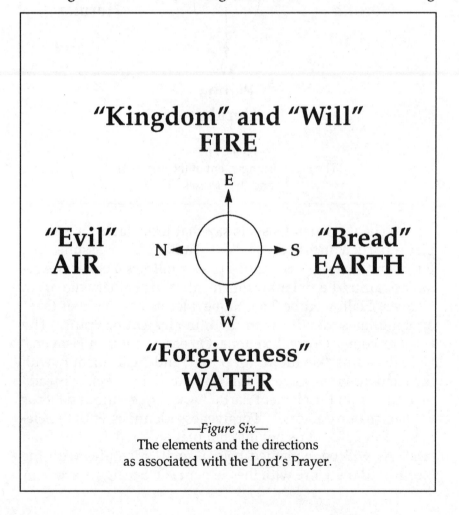

"Kingdom" and "Will"
FIRE

"Evil"
AIR

"Bread"
EARTH

"Forgiveness"
WATER

—*Figure Six*—
The elements and the directions
as associated with the Lord's Prayer.

pendulum associates certain basic concepts with cardinal points, elements and rates (length of the thread):

Ten inches	:	East, Fire, Red, Light, Sun.
Twenty inches	:	South, Earth, White, Heat, Life.
Thirty inches	:	West, Water, Green, Moon.
Forty inches	:	North, Air, Black, Cold, Death.

Graves and Hoult, 1980: 98

Furthermore, Lethbridge discovered that this system of rates is determined by the Earth's mass, and not by its magnetic field (Graves and Hoult, 1980: 99). Lethbridge's findings show the familiar *polar* arrangement of elements and cardinal points.

In a recent book, Doreen Valiente, former High Priestess of Gerald Gardner's coven, discusses Tom C.Lethbridge's attribution of colors to the cardinal points. Valiente points out that this is very close to the old Celtic attribution: red to the east, white to the south, grey or shadowy to the west and black to the north (Valiente, 1989: 125). In another context, Valiente points out that the term "Watchtowers" for the guardians of the four cardinal points, came from Elizabethan England and the work of John Dee and Edward Kelley, through the Golden Dawn, through Aleister Crowley, to Gerald Gardner and modern Witchcraft (Valiente, 1989: 64). She does not mention that Edward Kelley recorded his clairvoyant vision on a gold disk, now in the British museum. This gold disk has an engraving of the four Watchtowers, and mentions their color attributions: dark green in the east, red in the west, black in the south, and white in the north (Laycock, 1978: plate on p. 51). This is a *polar* arrangement of colors and cardinal points. Clairvoyants insist that there are mirror-inversions in the inner planes. If we transpose the colors allocated to the cardinal points in Kelley's gold disk, we get Lethbridge's polar attributions. Of course, Edward Kelley may have been familiar with the Celtic arrangement. However, my point is that Lethbridge's *polar* attribution of colors — red to the east, white to the south, green to the west, and black to the north — is not new, but quite ancient within the Western tradition.

Doreen Valiente discusses the sequential and polar attribution of elements to cardinal points. She tells us that Gardner obtained the sequential arrangement — air in the east, fire in the south, water in the west, and earth in the north — from the Golden Dawn. Furthermore, the Golden Dawn people claimed that these attributions came "from the nature of the prevailing winds from those quarters" in the British Isles (Valiente, 1989: 124). For a while, Valiente worked with a coven led by Robert Cochrane, who claimed to be a hereditary Witch. Cochrane used a polar arrangement: fire in the east, earth in the south, water in the west, and air in the north. Valiente suggests that Cochrane might have borrowed these attributions from the pendulum rates discovered by Tom C. Lethbridge (Valiente, 1989: 124–125). Although Valiente eventually rejected Robert Cochrane because of his authoritarianism and malevolent sense of humor, she acknowledges that his group worked a form of magic that was considerably more powerful than that found in Gardner's coven (Valiente, 1989: 104). My point is that as of 1989, a former High Priestess of Gerald Gardner's coven, acknowledges that a magical ritual with a *polar* arrangement of the elements is "more potent" than one with a sequential arrangement.

A choice between the sequential, counterclockwise arrangement of the elements on the cardinal points or a polar arrangement in terms of opposites, is a purely experiential, pragmatic issue. We must decide on the basis of what works best or generates the greater amount of power. On that criterion, we recommend the polar arrangement. East is Red, contains the element Fire, and is associated with the Sun. South is White, contains the element Earth, and is associated with Heat and Life. West is Green, contains the element Water, and is associated with the Moon. North is Black, contains the element Air, and is associated with Cold and Death. See figure seven.

On pragmatic ground, we recommend that the neo-shaman or ritual magician use this polar arrangement because it will help to produce greater shamanic or magical power.

PRACTICE ONE

To make experiential contact with the shamanic inner world, you will need a drum, or a good quality drumming tape, and a pair of rattles or maracas. The account that follows is substantially the same as that described by Michael Harner in his book *The Way of the Shaman* (Harner, 1982: 37–50, 83–88, 98–108), with a few additions. We recommend that the student obtain Harner's book and read it for further details.

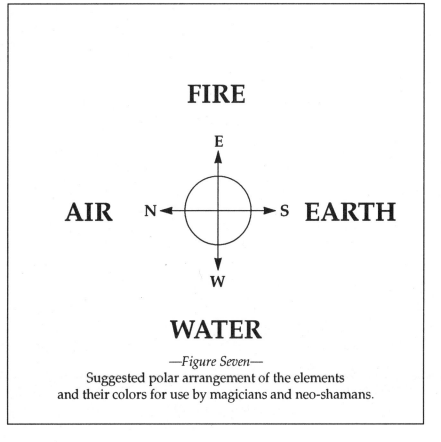

FIRE

AIR   N←⊕→S   **EARTH**

WATER

—*Figure Seven*—
Suggested polar arrangement of the elements
and their colors for use by magicians and neo-shamans.

In this first practice, we are going to teach you to do two things:

Calling the Power Animals: This is a brief shamanic ritual which uses the circle and the elements in a polar arrangement. Think of it as the remote ancestor of the circle in ritual magic.

Dancing the Animals: Here you will rattle and dance with or without the sound of a drum in the backround. You will be in darkness, with your eyes almost closed, and you will dance in free form and try to perceive the presence of an animal.

Comments:

1. A power animal is the archetype of the species. It is not a particular bear, but Bear, not a particular wolf, but Wolf. As archetypes, power animals are indestructible or immortal.

2. Power animals are wild, tameless animals. Pets or domesticated animals do not qualify. In the shamanic inner world, domesticated animals have no power.

3. Most of the time, insects do not qualify as power animals. They have power, but it is noxious to humans. However, this issue is ultimately context dependent. Michael Harner has pointed out that in rare contexts, insects need not represent disease (Harner, 1989: 2). Nevertheless, the pragmatic rule is that insects in a shamanic inner world tunnel or in the energy field of a person are etheric intrusions associated with disease or illness.

4. You accept any and all other animals as power animals. In the shamanic inner world, a gerbil is a good as a tiger, and just as powerful. Remember, the power animal is doing you, the human, a favor in coming to you.

5. Once you contact a power animal, you will start a relationship of reciprocity between two beings who are roughly

equal, but live in different dimensions. Through you and your dancing, the power animal re-experiences the sensations of living in a material body. In exchange, it makes its power and protection available to you.

Calling the Animals

You should be in a darkened room, preferably at night. Hold a rattle in each hand and almost close your eyes. Face East.

The East is Fire, and there you find the big predators such as lions, tigers, wolves, panthers, boars. Begin rattling with your right hand, in a zig-zag pattern from your knees to the top of your head and back again. As you rattle, whistle and mentally call the Fire animals. Do this for about two or three minutes, then turn to face the South.

The South is Earth and contains relatively peaceful, often vegetarian animals, such as bears, horses, apes or elephants. Rattle and whistle for two or three minutes, and mentally call the peaceful animals. Then turn West.

The West is Water, and there you find the animals that live in rivers, lakes, and oceans, such as fish, whales, squid, otters or seals. Rattle and whistle for two or three minutes and mentally call the animals that live in the water. Then turn to face North.

The North is Air and contains birds, such as eagles, falcons, and hawks. Rattle and whistle for two or three minutes and mentally call the animals that live in the air. Then turn to face East.

Rattle upward, briefly, toward the Sun, Moon, and stars. Then rattle downward for two or three minutes, mentally calling the spirit of planet Earth. Pause. Start jogging in place, rattling with both arms, mentally calling power animals from the four quarters. Do this for two or three minutes. Then use one hand to give a signal of four sharp rattles. This signal indicates the end of the ritual.

Comments:

The rattling is a monotonous sonic input that begins

to shift your awareness into the shamanic state of consciousness. In a sense, as you rattle to the quarters, you are calling the shamanic prototypes of the Watchtowers of ritual magic. Clairvoyant investigation reveals that whistling to the quarters brings an additional and very desirable energy.

Dancing the Animals

You are going to attempt your first contact with a power animal. For dancing, you may want a live drummer or a drumming tape, or no drum and just rattles. Experiment to find out what works best for you.

As soon as you finish calling the animals — while still in a darkened room with your eyes almost closed — begin to rattle and dance, moving in a general clockwise direction. Dance free-form, and try to let yourself go.

After a warm up of the first few minutes, you may begin to perceive an animal. This may be just a presence, or a feeling, or it may be an image or a series of images. Accept whatever you perceive and try to intensify the contact. You may feel like making the growls, cries, calls, or grunts of a particular animal. By all means do this out loud. You may feel like making the body movements of an animal. Go ahead and do so.

Somewhere along here your mood will begin to change toward the euphoria that is a characteristic of full shamanic consciousness. Once you have a power animal, you will be dancing that animal. At the end face East and use both rattles to rattle toward your chest four times, mentally welcoming your power animal.

The dancing should be done for a minimum of 15 minutes, and preferably longer. It must be repeated once a week on a regular basis.

You dance your power animal to raise shamanic power or energy. The dancing "feeds" or builds this energy. You need this power or energy for your own protection and to carry out the various shamanic operations in the inner planes. If the energy is not used, it leaves or dissipates. This is why it has to be built up again and again.

Comments:

People who are part of Western civilization usually feel silly at the idea of dancing an animal. This makes dancing your power animal on a regular, weekly basis, the boundary that separates serious practitioners from everybody else. The initial embarrassment will disappear as soon as you start to dance. Once you begin to experience the euphoria you will wonder how you could have lived without this experience. You will also have discovered a marvelous antidote against depression. Nothing is free. If you want to obtain shamanic power, you must work for it. In the next practice you will be taught how to journey to find your power animal.

CHAPTER TWO

THE
PSYCHOANALYTIC
CONTRIBUTION

We turn to 20th century psychoanalytic persuasions — in particular to those of Freud, Jung, Rank, and Grof — in search of insights that will explain some features of shamanism and the occult tradition, as well as some features of the historical religions.

SIGMUND FREUD

Sigmund Freud (1856–1939) discovered the human-animal unconscious with its twin libidinal drives of sex and aggression. In a sense, Freudian theory is about the tragic burden of our having evolved as predatory killer animals, somewhere in east Africa, about four million years ago. History shows that we are a dangerous, killer species, currently engaged in the extermination of other life forms. The daily round confirms that we must kill other living beings to feed and clothe ourselves and otherwise survive. In the late 20th century our aggression threatens to destroy us, through our military tech nology and through our devastation of the ecological infrastructure of the planet.

While inborn human aggression is a major focus of Freudian theory, his emphasis on sexuality has received greater exposure. This is because his theories surfaced at the end of both the Victorian era and at the end of 2000 years of Christian sexual repression and contempt for the body. As Nietzsche said, "Christianity gave Eros a poisoned cup. He did not die of it. He only turned into vice."

The sexual/aggressive libido lives according to the *pleasure principle:* the demand for immediate gratification. To survive, however, we develop an *ego.* The ego deals with the external world and tries to live according to the reality principle. This ego is equipped with mechanisms of defense (rationalization, repression, projection, introjection, displacement, condensation, idealization), which only illustrate another Nietzschean aphorism: "The measure of a man is how much truth he can withstand." The answer is, "not much."

Through parents and others, we internalize the symbols, ideals, prohibitions, and superstitions of our culture. This forms the punitive superego, the Trojan horse of society within the citadel of the self. From this point on, guilt, anxiety, and the drives to achieve and conform will make their contributions to our normal unhappiness. Society exists but at a price: the human being is a sick animal.

We grow through stages of psychosexual development. An oral phase, in which the crawling child will try to ingest anything, will later manifest as adult oral needs (verbal self-expression, kissing, alcoholism). In the anal phase the child uses feces to negotiate with the parents, and thus we learn gift-giving and money-hoarding. Retention causes pain but provides leverage and the sweetness of power: here we find the roots of adult sadism and masochism. The Protestant puritan ethic, with its obsessive cleanliness and drive to save and accumulate, expressed sublimated anal needs. Painters smear walls and flat surfaces. Sculptors play with feces in a sublimated mode. Rodin's "The Thinker" is a man having a bowel movement. And the esthetic ensemble below him, namely, the "Gates of Hell," confirm this: the figures of the damned are distinctly fecal and hell is a projection of anal sadism.

The widespread prohibition against incest points to that which it forbids: the incest wish. Behind the incest wish we find the desire to return to the womb. We desire to return to the womb because we once spent nine months in a completely protected environment in which all our needs were instantly gratified. The maternal womb is the original pattern for all religious conceptions of paradise or heaven.

The incest wish (and its prohibition) explains much in human culture. Christians are fascinated by their dogmas of the Trinity and the virginity of Mary, so that Jesus can be his own father. Through the entire length of Shakespeare's tragedy, Hamlet is unable to kill Claudius because Claudius has fulfilled Hamlet's own most forbidden wish: he has killed Hamlet's father and married Hamlet's mother.

The child idealizes both parents, but particularly the parent of the opposite sex. At the adult interpersonal level, this idealization provides the pattern for the desired love-object and for the phenomenon of transference. As Freud said, in every man-woman relationship there are four people: the man, the woman, his mother, and her father.

Parental idealization also produces the gods. Male gods are idealized father images. Goddesses are idealized mother images. The religions of faith promote infantilism because they reduce adults to the status of children.

Freudian dream symbolism is of boring simplicity: the counters are limited to male sex symbols (swords, knives, guns, lances, towers, trees), female sex symbols (caves, houses, churches, purses), intercourse symbols (going up or down stairs), incest wishes, and murderous aggression. But there is also much wisdom. Freud taught that we grow like onions; we add layers but the child remains at the center. Because of this, happiness is the satisfaction of a childhood wish.

When Freudian theory is applied to shamanism, it is obvious that the shamanic altered state of consciousness is some kind of regression and involves libidinal gratification. But it is regression in the service of the ego, because it strengthens the personality and increases our ability to cope with external reality. The Freudian outlook decodes two of our prime symbols. The World Tree is a male penis or phallic symbol. The World Mountain is a womb-vagina symbol. Since our bodies are one of our few intimate possessions, it is only appropriate that we should use them to symbolize the cosmos to ourselves.

CARL JUNG AND OTTO RANK

Certain landmarks in the life of *Carl Jung* (1875–1961) stand out as influences on his later discoveries. Sexually explicit dreams led him to ask: if you dream of a tree, it is a phallic symbol; but if you dream of an erect penis, what does that symbolize? There had to be another level to dream and myth symbolism. In 1900 Jung wrote a thesis in psychiatry for the University of Leipzig. It was a study of a girl cousin who was a medium or channel. Jung theorized that the psyche can split into many semi-autonomous fragments and that mental health or wholeness involves reintegration.

His brief association with Freud (1910–1913) was followed by a period of breakdown, isolation and visionary experience. In 1916 he experienced a three-day visionary sequence in which he saw and heard Basilides of Alexandria (a leader of the ancient Gnostics) arrive at his house and preach seven sermons to the dead. From this point on, Gnostic ideas about opposites will have an important place in his system.

The story about how Jung discovered synchronicity has been told many times. A male analysand came for his appointed hour, complained of a mild sore throat, and then left. Hours later, the man's wife phoned Jung to ask if her husband was dead. Why did she ask that? Because pigeons had flocked to her window. This had happened only once before in her life, when her father died. Unknown to both Jung and the man's wife, the man had dropped dead of a heart attack at the precise moment that the pigeons arrived at the window. The arrival of pigeons does not cause human deaths and human deaths do not attract pigeons. Yet, the arrival of pigeons at her window had communicated a unit of correct information to the dead man's wife. From this, and similar bizarre experiences, Jung concluded that there must be an acausal link in the universe. He called this synchronicity. Later on he suggested that astrology is a case of synchronicity.

Jung discovered a vast new realm of the unconscious which is shared by animals and humans. He called this realm the *collective unconscious* because it is not part of us. Rather, we are part of it. The collective unconscious is a domain of creative imagination that contains much knowledge and wisdom. It is inhabited by archetypes (gods, goddesses, and mythical patterns). It contains the pantheons of all religions. At the individual human level, the collective unconscious contains the archetypes called the *animus*, the *anima*, and the *shadow*.

The anima is the psychological feminine which is usually repressed from male consciousness. In male dreams it appears as a young woman. In behavior it manifests as sentimentality, and male inability to handle feelings. The animus is the psychological masculine which is usually repressed from female consciousness. In female dreams it appears as a male figure. In behavior it manifests as bitchiness and female inability to handle authority and power.

Some dreams are purely Freudian dreams. Some dreams are only Jungian dreams. And some dreams are both Freudian and Jungian. The latter allow us to sort out the symbolism.

Consider the following dream remembered by a very attractive and feminine woman in her mid-20s: At age 10 or 11 she had a recurrent dream in which a man stabbed her to death with a knife. At a Freudian level, the preadolescent girl both fears and perhaps looks forward to sexual intercourse. The Jungian level is equally obvious. At age 10 or 11 this person was living in such a way that her animus was "killing" or overwhelming the rest of her personality. The adult woman smiled in surprise: "You would never imagine what a tomboy I used to be at that time." The Jungian advice is to become whole by accepting and integrating the animus or the anima.

One of the more dramatic archetypes is the shadow, defined as *that which we have rejected and refuse to acknowledge.* Shadow dreams are fear, terror, and persecution dreams. The pursuer, if not a blob, force, or monster, must have the same gender as the dreamer. In his book *Answer to Job,* Jung examined the biblical dialogue between Job and Jehova. He argues that Job holds the moral high ground because he has seen the shadow of Jehova (murderous aggression). The analysis can be extended to the gospels. The portrayal of Jesus is that of a noble, mystical being devoid of the Freudian libido — completely lacking in sexual and aggressive drives. So, where do we find the sexuality and aggression of Jesus? They have been removed to make up the Christian Satan. For Satan is just that: unconscious (and therefore primitive) aggression and sexuality.

There are creation myths, cosmic destruction myths, and journey of the hero myths. There are father archetypes (the magician, the tyrant, the wise old man) and mother archetypes (the earth mother, the goddess, the devouring or terrible mother) and transformation archetypes (the night sea journey). The organizing center of the collective unconscious is the archetype of the self. The Jungian self is not the ego, but something like the Tao or an impersonal god. Health and wholeness involve a quest in which the ego tries to get beyond the opposites and establish a relationship with the self. In dreams the self appears as the *quaternio,* a circle divided at four points or into four parts. In religious art its best exemplars are Buddhist Tibetan mandalas or some rose windows in several Gothic cathedrals. Jung was very fond of the hexagrams of the *I Ching* and of the Tarot trumps. He regarded these mantic devices as descriptions and portraits of archetypes.

For Jung, the archetypes are "psychoid," which means that they have a direct (synchronistic) impact on the external world, an impact that bypasses individual ego consciousness. However, individual consciousness can visit the archetypes by carrying out inner journeys in an altered state of consciousness. Jung called these journeys *active imagination*. Active imagination journeys involve surprise, promote wholeness, and are the opposite of day dreaming.

Jungian theory has a particular affinity with shamanism and the esoteric tradition. The World Tree and the World Mountain stand in a circle, which is guarded at the four cardinal points, at the center of the world. This early version of the circle of ritual magic is an obvious expression of the *quaternio*, or the archetype of the self. Shamanic inner journeys are the use of active imagination to explore the collective unconscious and promote wholeness. Synchronicity explains how a purely inner world operation, carried out in an altered state of consciousness, can change something in the objective external world. Shamanic divination and the later mantic methods (*I Ching*, Geomancy, Tarot) are probes that often succeed in tapping the wisdom and knowledge of the collective unconscious. The teachers found in the shamanic Upper World are archetypal deities. Some of the demonic or angry spirits found in the Middle World are shadow figures. Finally, Gnostic ideas about the opposites have been very influential in shaping both Jungian theory and the occult tradition.

For *Otto Rank* (1884–1939), Freud's protegee and disciple, human birth is horrendously traumatic and a major source of both anxiety and neurosis. In his book *The Trauma of Birth*, he argued that the birth trauma has to be re-experienced in therapy for any serious healing to take place. Though rejected by the rest of the psychoanalytic movement, this insight came into its own half a century later.

STANISLAV GROF

In our day, the clinical research on LSD by psychiatrist *Stanislav Grof*, has produced an enlarged map of the unconscious as made up of three domains: a Freudian unconscious, a Rankian unconscious, and a Jungian collective unconscious (Grof, 1988: 45-160). Grof's initial data base was made up of 2500 LSD sessions, at more than five hours per session, from a population of Czech and American patients. In addition, he had access to the records from 1300 more sessions run by other Czech and American psychiatrists (Grof, 1975: 14). Analysis of this body of 3800 LSD clinical sessions revealed that about a third of the material contained Freudian themes (i.e., sexual symbolism). Another third contained Jungian themes (i.e., mythical patterns and feelings of religious transcendence). The remaining third were scenes of suffering, pain, torture, hopelessness, and the death-rebirth experience associated with successful passage through the birth canal. In other words, Grof discovered that a Rankian birth-trauma unconscious exists side by side with a Freudian unconscious, and a Jungian collective unconscious.

Further investigation allowed Grof to specify the Rankian birth-trauma unconscious as four Perinatal Matrices. In LSD sessions, the phenomenology of these matrices is as follows:

1. Before the onset of labor: feelings of cosmic unity and ecstasy;

2. As contractions begin: feelings of enormous and endless pain and suffering, feelings of hopelessness and engulfment;

3. Intensified pain and suffering, explosions, feelings of destruction by fire, tortures, sacrifices, battles, sexual and ,sadomasochistic orgies, the experience of dying;

4. Feelings of rebirth and release following the successful passage through the birth canal (Grof, 1988: 11-29, 301).

As Grof points out, the Perinatal Matrices of the Rankian birth-trauma unconscious explain the torment and hellfire visions of some historical religions such as Christianity or Tibetan Buddhism. Furthermore, the Perinatal Matrices contain the death-rebirth experience. This means that quite aside from the winter-spring vegetation cycle, these matrices explain the death-rebirth theme of classical shamanism (Eliade, 1964: 33-64), and the pattern of dying gods (e.g., Osiris, Christ) of historical religions.

The extent to which psychoanalytic investigations explain portions of core shamanism and shamanic themes in historical religions can be seen in the following table:

PSYCHOLOGY AND SHAMANISM		
Grof	**Core Shamanism**	**Shamanic Themes in Religions**
Perinatal Matrices	Dismemberment	Hell-fire visions
Birth-Trauma (Rank)	Death-Rebirth	Dying Gods: Osiris, Christ
Psychodynamic (Freud)	World Tree World Mountain	Trees in Eden Sinai, Mt.Meru the Ziggurat
Transcendental (Jung)	Quaternio	Four Evangelists Four Children of Horus
	Teachers	Gods/Goddesses

When we turn to the shamanic inner world, we see that the World Tree or the World Mountain gives the shaman access to three regions and their multiple levels. The Lower World is the home of the power animals. The Middle World contains unpleasant, fearful, lost, or negative spirits, and records of past lives. The Upper World contains teachers in human form, cross-culturally identified as gods and goddesses. Thousands of years later, the Western occult tradition describes two inner regions, the Lower Astral and the Upper Astral. Part of the Lower Astral reflects the "raw sexuality and murderous aggression of human beings. As a domain, it is both dangerous and distinctly unpleasant" (Brennan, 1971: 86). The Upper Astral contains gods and goddesses, highly evolved entities, and is far beyond the human level. These descriptions of inner world geography can be compared.

SHAMANIC AND OCCULT WORLDS	
Shamanic Inner World	**Occult Inner World**
Upper World Teachers in human form	*Upper Astral* Gods and Goddesses
Middle World Unpleasant, fearful, lost spirits	*Lower Astral* negative emotions
Surface of the Earth	
Lower World Power Animals	

As this comparison shows, both descriptions are descriptions of the same inner world. The major difference is that, with the exception of traditions such as that of the Witch's familiar, the Western occult tradition has forgotten about the Lower World and its extraordinary power animals. Furthermore, the Middle World (or Lower Astral) partly corresponds to the Rankian birth-trauma unconscious, while the Upper World (or Upper Astral) roughly corresponds to the Jungian collective unconscious.

An alternative model makes use of the metaphor of the center and the periphery. The center contains the more physical energy of the power animals while the periphery contains the more spiritual energy of the guides or teachers in human form. Since we live in a physical body, the further out we go without returning to the center, the more likely we are to get weak or sick. Some psychics seem to be in this condition. If you stay at the center you increase your physical vitality, but receive no spiritual energy. Clearly, a human being needs a balance of both kinds of energy. This suggests that our shamanic journeys should give approximately equal time to Upper World and Lower World activities. It makes sense to take your power animal on Upper World journeys.

PRACTICE TWO

We are going to teach you how to journey to the Lower World to find your power animal. You will be lying down on your back, head pointed to the North or East, with arms and legs uncrossed. You should be wearing a blindfold and have your eyes closed. This should be done in darkness — preferably at night. Disconnect the phone and insure privacy. Depending on season and climate, use a blanket or wear warm socks. It is important that your feet not get cold. You will need a live drummer or the sound of a drumming tape. The drumming tape should have a "return signal" at the end. This can be a superimposed alternative sound or four sharp taps and accelerated drumming. If you are using a live drummer, have him/her give the return signal after 15 or 20 minutes.

The shamanic Lower World is a sector of the Astral plane. The Astral plane is made up of powerful psychic energies that are given shape by the imagination. So stop worrying about "I feel that I am imagining this, or making it happen." It makes no difference. At first you might be making it happen, but if you persist, the experience will take off on its own. Eventually, you will experience the two unmistakable signs that your conscious ego is not making it happen and that you have entered the shamanic state of consciousness: you will begin to experience euphoria or joy and you will experience surprise at inner world events.

To journey to the Lower World you need a point of departure that actually exists in the ordinary world. You need this in order to establish a clear boundary between ordinary and non-ordinary reality. Crossing this boundary will produce an important shift in awareness. This point of departure can be a natural cave, a hot spring, or even the roots of a huge tree.

You begin by remembering—visualizing your point of departure and establishing inner sensory awareness. Touch the walls of your cave. What are the colors? What is the ground like? Smell the air. What is the temperature? If you are using a hot spring or the inside of a root of a tree, do the same thing. Then imagine a tunnel leading downward. Is there some light in the tunnel? Touch the walls. Begin moving into the tunnel. You can walk, run, or slide. Let the sound of the drum propel you forward.

Some people just flow downward at top speed. Feet first, head first, it does not matter. Do whatever feels comfortable. Once you are in the tunnel, look ahead and begin hunting for an exit which usually appears as a point of light. If you see it, head for it. If you have trouble finding an exit, then go ahead and imagine an exit as a point of light and head for it.

As soon as you come out, establish sensory awareness. Where are you? Is it desert, a jungle or meadow? Are there any mountains? Is there any water? What is the ground like? Is it warm or cold? Is it day or night? Can you locate the Sun or the Moon? Can you guess the time? What season is it? What sounds do you hear? Smell the air. Touch the rocks and plants.

At this point, stand up (in your shamanic inner world), open your arms and call out "Will my power animal please come to me." Repeat this two or three times while scanning the scene from side to side, looking for signs of animal life and motion. An animal may come to you. If nothing happens, then begin walking. You are searching for your power animal. As you walk, pause and call out, and continue to scan.

Eventually, you will encounter an animal. Here the rule is that you must see it four times (e.g., the close-up of an eye, a medium shot from the rear, the view of a foot, a close-up of the head). Then you face the animal and ask "Are you my power animal?" You will get some kind of answer: a verbal response, a nod or gesture, or no answer. If the answer is negative or you get no answer, then thank the animal and continue the search.

It is not unusual to encounter several animals until one acknowledges that he/she is your power animal. When this finally happens, it is common to feel a wave of affection for the animal, and to want to touch it and hug it. By all means do so. Thank the animal for having come to you to be your power animal. Then visit with your power animal. While you visit, you may want to ask your power animal to give you a song, call, sound, or signal by which you can establish immediate contact or call it to come to you in an emergency.

At some point during your visit, the drum will give the return signal. Say goodbye to your power animal, go back to your tunnel, and return to the ordinary world. Then get up and write down your experience. Do this immediately, and before talking to anyone, because partial amnesia ensues very quickly and you lose details. You are still coming back from an altered state of consciousness, so give yourself a few minutes to re-establish contact with the ordinary world. You may want to have a bite of food or something to drink, as this helps earthing or grounding in ordinary reality. It would be very unwise to immediately rush out and drive your car.

Calling the animals at the cardinal points, dancing your power animal, and journeying, constitute basic shamanic practice which must be done on a weekly basis. As you practice, you will notice that shamanic power begins to manifest in your life as good luck, positive synchronicities, and reasonable immunity to feelings of depression and loneliness. While nothing can guarantee complete safety, shamanic power will also increase protection against illness and accidents.

It is a trade-off. You do shamanic practice to get these benefits. However, even with faithful weekly practice, your power animal will eventually get restless and leave you (Harner, 1982: 125–126). In our experience, this happens after two or three years. The departing power animal may pass you on to another power animal and return at intervals to check on you and see how you are doing. Furthermore, by then you may well have several power animals. Some of these will come and go, while others will remain for longer periods. We would like to suggest that changing power animals can be understood as a sign of personal growth: you have learned one set of lessons or you are ready for new experiences.

As a general rule, the identity of your power animal should be kept secret from all those who are not engaged in shamanic work. Unnecessary talk about your power animal makes you lose power. If you boast, your power animal is likely to leave you. In this domain the rule is discretion and humility. Remember that you are not the source of the power.

What is the identity of your power animal? The nature of your power animal will indicate an element. If your power animal is a wolf, a leopard, or a tiger, this indicates the element fire, and its associated traits of leadership, courage, and aggression. If your power animal is an otter, a seal, or a sea turtle, this indicates the element water, and its corresponding emphasis on feelings and nurturing abilities. An elephant or a wild horse, indicates the element earth and its associated qualities of stability, common sense, and practicality. If your power animal is a bird, this indicates the element air and a more intellectual focus. There are combinations. An eagle or a hawk would indicate air and fire or aggressive intellect. A sea gull would point to air and water or intellect and feeling. The element-identity of your power animal may point to your strongest trait, or it may indicate an area of weakness where you are deficient and need help. Eventually, as your shamanic practice extends over months and years, you are likely to obtain several power animals.

Enhancing Techniques:

You have learned how to enter the inner planes of the occult tradition or the shamanic inner world. So long as you are in the company of your power animal, you can now journey anywhere in this domain with complete safety. We are now going to teach you a few ways to enhance shamanic dancing and journeying.

1. Did your power animal give you a call or signal by which you can make immediate contact? If so, then incorporate this call or signal when you dance your power animal. Also, while dancing, as soon as you begin to perceive your power animal, increase the tempo of dancing and rattling. Try to dance for 15 minutes.

2. There is a preparatory technique, adapted from a non-shamanic source, which seems to enhance access to the shamanic state of consciousness. As such, we recommend that you try it after dancing, but before journeying. It is as follows:

   a. Massage your feet and ankles (two minutes).

   b. Lie down, make a fist, and using the soft flesh adjacent to the little finger, massage your forehead over the area of the third eye (one minute).

   c. Use the fingertips of both hands to massage your temples in a circular motion (one minute).

   d. Relax, arms to the sides, eyes closed. Imagine that your feet and ankles are extending by two inches. Then imagine that your head and neck are extending by two inches. Then imagine that your feet and ankles are extending by 12 inches. Then imagine that your head and neck are extending by 12 inches. Then imagine that your feet and ankles are extending by 48 inches. Then imagine that your head and neck are extending by 48 inches. (These extensions are often signalled by definite feelings.)

   e. Expand your aura until it fills the room.

   f. Visualize yourself standing on the roof of your house. Face East. Describe to yourself what you see. Turn clockwise to the South. Describe to yourself what you see. Turn to the West. Describe to yourself what you see. Turn to the North. Describe to yourself what you see. Return to face East. (At some point during this clock wise turn, you are likely to feel an almost irresistible impulse to float upwards. For the time being, resist that impulse, and force yourself back on to your roof).

Glaskin, 1974: 178–180

3. In all shamanic journeys, the intensity of the experience can be enhanced by using the technique of simultaneous narration invented by Michael Harner (Harner in Dore: 1988: 179–187). Proceed as follows:

   a. Use earphones and a drumming tape in a cassette player.

   b. At the same time, set up a tape recorder and a microphone.

   c. As you journey, verbally narrate out loud everything that happens during the journey. Doing this intensifies the experience to a remarkable degree (Dore, 1990–91: 8).

   d. At the end of your journey, you can play back the tape, and catch important details and information that might have already vanished due to a certain amount of instant amnesia.

CHAPTER THREE

ON THE KABBALAH

From the point of view of shaman-
ism, the Kabbalah is a particularly elaborate version of the
World Tree (and not a diagram of the psychology of a monotheistic deity). We scanned the traditions of the more ancient
and coherent Jewish Kabbalah and the newer Christian version in search of techniques that might enhance the activities
of contemporary neo-shamans and ritual magicians. This
viewpoint will have some consequences for what we retain
and what we discard, and for our evaluation of the history of
the Kabbalah.

A very provisional definition of Kabbalah might be to
say that it is a body of Gnostic doctrines, mystical practices,
visionary procedures and theurgic or magical rituals which
developed within Judaism until the 16th century. Furthermore, in 15th century Italy, some of these procedures and rituals were recast in a Christian framework. The Jewish Kabbalah
came to be identified as the esoteric doctrine of Judaism while
the Christian Kabbalah became a major focus of Western occultism, from the Renaissance magicians to the Hermetic

Order of the Golden Dawn in the last decade of Victorian England.

The surviving texts of Jewish Kabbalah run into the thousands, mostly as unpublished, and sometimes anonymous, manuscripts. Of those that have been published, three stand out as particularly influential:

a. *Sefer Yetzirah* or *Book of Formation*, from the second or third century C.E.

b. The *Bahir*, which appeared c. 1170 C.E., in Southern France, and was attributed to Rabbi Isaac the Blind, although it probably came to Provence from the Middle East.

c. The *Zohar* or *Book of Splendor*, which appeared in Spain c.1280 C.E. and was probably written by rabbi Moses de Leon.

The *Sefer Yetzirah* is a pamphlet of a few pages. The *Bahir* is a slender book. The current Hebrew edition of the *Zohar* runs to 22 volumes.

Contemporary scholarship on the Kabbalah, still dominated by the work of the late Gershom Scholem and his disciples, tends to consider the *Sefer Yetzirah* a pre-Kabbalah text, for two reasons:

1. The *Sefer Yetzirah* appeared in the Middle East in the second or third century C.E., and then nothing else seems to happen for eight or nine centuries. In contrast, the *Bahir* and the *Zohar* are part of the very creative period of Kabbalistic activity in Provence, Castille, and Catalonia, in the 12th and 13th centuries.

2. In the *Sefer Yetzirah*, the *sefirot* (numbers) and the 22 mystical consonants of the Hebrew alphabet are *external* to the Jewish deity. In the *Bahir* and in the *Zohar* the *sefirot* and the 22 consonants are *internal* attributes of Jehovah; or as one writer has put it, they are the internal parts of the psychology of God (Blumenthal, 1978: 114).

We disagree with this learned opinion. Since we are not concerned with championing monotheism, we feel that any text which is focused on the dynamics of the sefirot and the 22 mystical consonants is a text of the Kabbalah. By this criterion, the *Sefer Yetzirah* is the first text of the Kabbalah. It does make a difference. If you exclude the *Sefer Yetzirah*, then the Kabbalah begins in the 12th century in Southern France and Spain. If you include the *Sefer Yetzirah*, then the Kabbalah begins in the second or third centuries C.E. in the Middle East.

The historical sources of the Kabbalah seem to be as follows:

1. *Jewish Monotheism*, and the mysticism of the 22 consonants of the Hebrew alphabet.

2. *Jewish Merkabah* or Chariot mysticism, from c. 538 B.C.E. These writings, which include the *Book of Enoch* and the *Hekhalot* books, describe visionary journeys by mystics who brave hostile forces to visit the seven heavenly palaces and the flaming throne of Jehovah. As Scholem has pointed out, *Merkabah* visionary journeys are thoroughly Gnostic (Scholem, 1941: 49).

3. *Gnosticism:* The entire set of problems raised by the Gnostic schools (c. 50 C.E. – 300 C.E.) is found in the Kabbalah. As Scholem says, the early Kabbalah was almost entirely Gnostic (Scholem, 1941: 117). This most original ingredient will be discussed separately.

4. *Neo-Platonism:* This current, with its emphasis on the importance of the feminine, became an influence on the 12th and 13th century Kabbalah of Spain and Southern France, and was a major influence on the Christian Kabbalah of the Renaissance.

These are the main historical sources, but there is a fifth ingredient which is often ignored precisely because it is not an historical source. As we shall see, the Kabbalah organizes the sefirot and the 22 mystical consonants into a *Tree of Life*. This tree is none other than a version of the World Tree of shamanism.

An examination of the historical sources of the Kabbalah reveals "Judaism" and "Gnosticism." These two ingredients are in contradiction or opposition on almost every issue. Gnosticism is dualistic or polytheistic, while Judaism is monotheistic. Gnosticism is emanational, while Judaism is creationist. Gnosticism champions gender parity, and therefore the cause of the feminine, while Judaism is mostly patriarchal. The Kabbalah manages to combine these contradictory emphases, in dynamic tension and uneasy balance.

Like shamanism, Gnosticism is anarchistic (Lacarriere, 1977: 51, 71). Therefore, there was no Gnostic orthodoxy. Instead, Gnosticism appeared as a multitude of sects led by visionaries like Basilides of Alexandria or magicians like Simon Magus. Nevertheless, the various Gnostic sects were unified by a focus on similar concerns. All Gnostics were concerned with the problem of opposites in human life and in the cosmos. All Gnostics were concerned with how, at death, the divine human spark can bypass the evil lower gods or planetary spirits and return to its source.

Gnostic concern with the problem of opposites focused on two issues: the femaleness of God or of the gods, and the problem of evil. Gnostic sense of justice demanded gender parity. The gods, all the way up to the primal Source, are organized into male and female, or as male-female in dynamic harmony (Pagels, 1981: 59, 61). Unless it is used to inflict pain, suffering, or destructive aggression, human sexual behavior is not evil and is of no concern to the cosmic powers. Basilides said that all acts of human voluptuousness are a subject of complete indifference to the gods (Lacarriere, 1977: 54).

The problem of evil is more complicated. For the Gnostics, evil is cruelty, sadism, violence, torture, slaughter and massacres: destructive surplus aggression. They found this evil not only in human history but also in nature — in that organized cruelty, sadism and violence which Darwinians call natural selection and the survival of the fittest (Lacarriere, 1977: 24).

In the teachings of the first great Gnostic, Simon Magus, and in that of the last, Marcion, we find a common dualistic cosmology. A nature organized so that one species will torture, kill and feed on another, and a human history made up of massacres and oppression, can only be the work of a partly evil creator demiurge. They identified this demiurge with the angry Jehovah of the Bible, and argued that there must exist a remote God of love and goodness who is a stranger to this world. This dualistic scheme was amplified by Saturninus into a hierarchy of partly evil Archons or planetary spirits that mediate between the remote good God and the evil creator God (Lacarriere, 1977: 46–51, 58, 100).

In modern terms, the Gnostic paradox of evil can be stated simply. History and nature exhibit organized cruelty and wanton suffering inflicted on countless creatures. Since humans evolved from other animals, human destructive aggression is animal destructive aggression refined by human intelligence. Who is responsible for this arrangement? If you assume that there is only one God, then you have a problem. If he is all-good, then he cannot be all-powerful. If he is all-powerful, then he has to be partly evil. In his *Theodicy*, the philosopher Leibniz (1646–1716) reached a similar conclusion. Within monotheism, the only possible logical solution for the problem of evil requires the principles of both good and evil to coexist in the one God (Scholem, 1987: 127).

There were Christian Gnostics (e.g., Marcion), Jewish Gnostics (the *Merkabah* mystics), and pagan Gnostics (e.g., the authors of the *Corpus Hermeticum*, c. 2nd century C.E.). Persecuted by the Roman Empire and by organized Christianity, they were eventually exterminated or went underground. However, sometime in the 2nd or 3rd century C.E., Gnostic ideas resurfaced to make up the Jewish Kabbalah.

The Kabbalah is made up of 10 (and eventually 11) sefirot and the 22 mystical consonants of the Hebrew alphabet. In this arrangement, the sefirot are powers and the 22 consonants are deployed as *paths* between them. Our synchronic, non-historical presentation of the Jewish Kabbalah must begin with the sefirot. See figure eight.

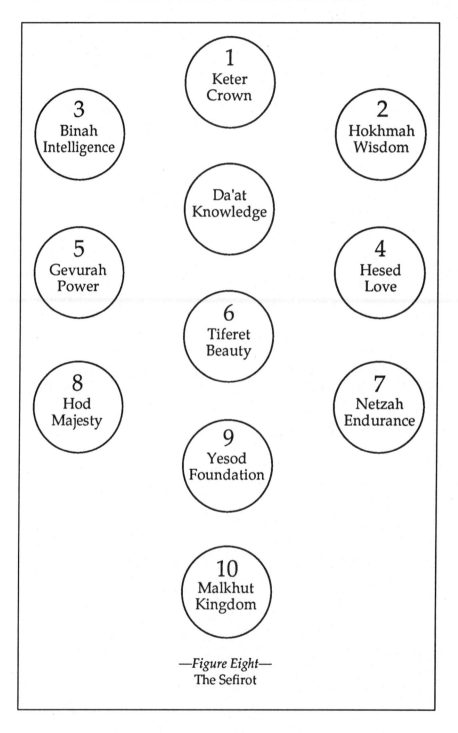

—*Figure Eight*—
The Sefirot

Since number ten (Malkhut) is eventually identified as planet Earth, the sefirot are none other than a Jewish version of the Archons or planetary spirits of the Gnostics. Gender parity, another Gnostic concern, is also included. Number one (Keter) is purely masculine. Number ten (Malkhut) is purely feminine. The other sefirot are both masculine and feminine. There is an eleventh sefira (Da'at or Knowledge) which has no number. This is said to be a hidden sefira. Behind number one (Keter) is *Ain Soph Aur* or "the limitless light." Behind Ain Soph Aur is *Ain Soph* or "the limitless." And behind Ain Soph is *Ain* or "nothingness." The ultimate source of the Kabbalah is an entity called "Nothingness," and this brings us very close to the cosmology of Tibetan Buddhism where the primal Source is the union of Emptiness and Bliss

Number one (Keter) is *Arikh Anpin* or the Vast Countenance. He is also called "serene" and "long suffering." Number one is an approximate equivalent of the remote good God of the Gnostics. Sefirot numbers four, five, six, seven, eight, and nine, make up *Zair Anpin,* or the Small Countenance. The Small Countenance is also called "impatient" and "short tempered." In the *Zohar* it says that through the sefirot on the right column [2, 4, 7] he gives life, and through the sefirot on the left column [3, 5, 8] he kills (*Zohar*, Sperling, Simon, Levertoff trans., 1934 : vol. 1, par. 22b, p. 93). The Small Countenance seems to be an approximate equivalent of the demiurge of the Gnostics. As the authors of the Kabbalah attempt to deal with the problem of evil, Gnostic dualism reappears.

In chapters II through V, the *Sefer Yetzirah* calls attention to the internal divisions of the Hebrew alphabet. Aleph, Mem, and Shin are the three Mother letters, identified with the elements Air, Water, and Fire. These make up the three horizontal paths of the Kabbalah, the paths that link the benevolent right side with the sinister left side. See figure nine.

This diagram has a probable error or transposition between Aleph (Air) and Shin (Fire). Aleph (Air) should be the horizontal between sefirot two and three. Shin (Fire) should

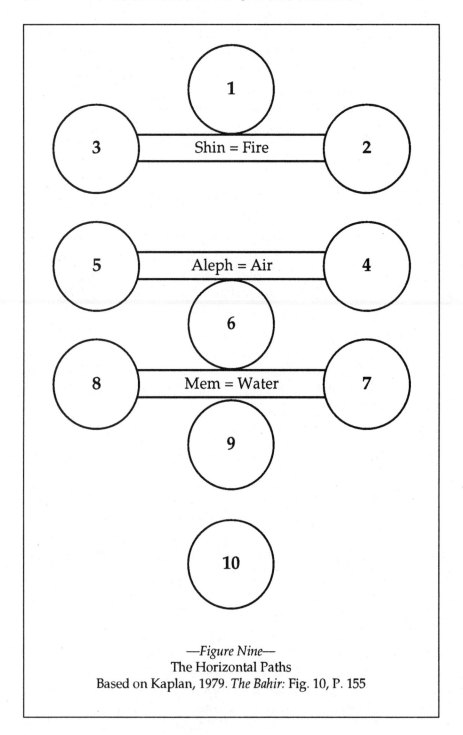

—*Figure Nine*—
The Horizontal Paths
Based on Kaplan, 1979. *The Bahir:* Fig. 10, P. 155

be the horizontal between sefirot four and five. The normal order of the elements arranged in horizontal bands from the bottom up are Earth (sefira ten), Water (sefirot seven, eight, and nine), Fire (sefirot four, five, and six), and Air (sefirot two, three, and Da'at, which has no number).

The seven double letters, so called because they have two sounds associated with each, are Beth, Gimel, Daleth, Kaph, Pe, Resh, and Tav. These letters are associated with qualities, directions, orifices of the body, days of the week, and planets. They make up the vertical paths of the Kabbalah. See figure ten.

The 12 simple letters are He, Vau, Zain, Heth, Teth, Yod, Lamed, Nun, Samek, Ayin, Tzaddi, and Qoph. They are associated with organs, senses, psychological properties, directions, and the signs of the zodiac. They make up the diagonal paths of the Kabbalah. The diagonals from the right side are He (Aries), Zain (Gemini), Teth (Leo), Heth (Cancer), Yod (Virgo), and Nun (Scorpio). The diagonals from the left side (in inverse order) are Lamed (Libra), Samek (Saggitarius), Tzaddi (Aquarius), Ayin (Capricorn), Qoph (Pisces), and Vau (Taurus). The point here is that the two sets of diagonals are arranged in terms of zodiacal oppositions or polarities. See figure eleven.

The column on the right (sefirot two, four, seven) is ruled by the element Water. The column on the left (sefirot three, five, and eight) is ruled by the element Fire. The column in the middle, or "Middle Pillar" (sefirot one, Da'at, six, nine, and ten), is ruled by the element Air. As the *Sefer Yetzirah* says, Air is a tongue of balance between Water and Fire (*Sefer Yetzirah*, 1975: Ch.II, Sec.I). We can now look at the combination of sefirot with horizontal, vertical, and diagonal paths, that make up the Jewish Kabbalah. See figure twelve.

In the *Bahir, evil is an attribute of God.* Evil is identified with the destructive aggression of sefira number five, Geburah, on the left hand column.

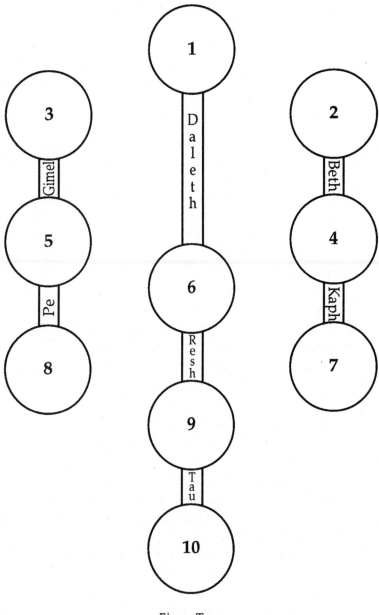

—*Figure Ten*—
The Vertical Paths

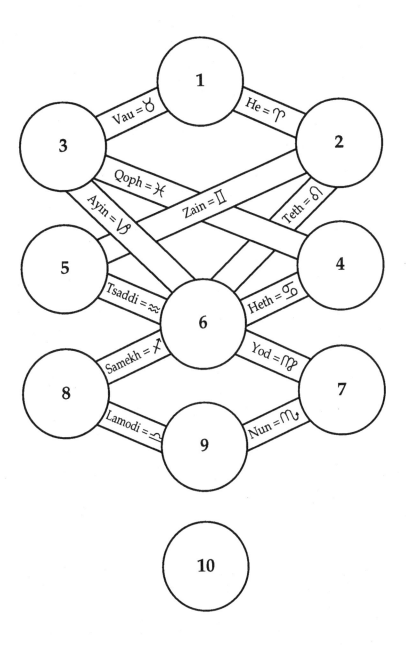

—*Figure Eleven*—
The Diagonal Paths

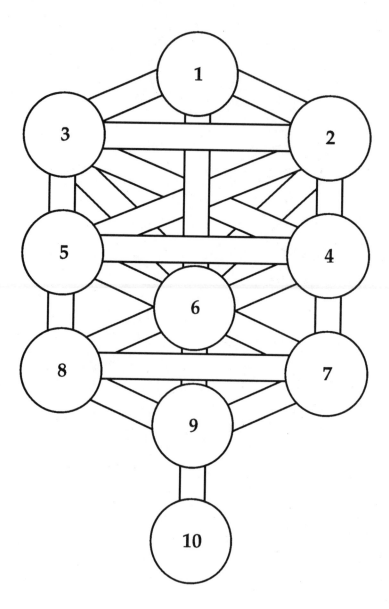

—*Figure Twelve*—
The Jewish Tree of Life

*This teaches us that the Blessed Holy One has
an Attribute whose name is Evil. It is to the
North of the Blessed Holy One, as it is written
(Jeremiah 1:14),"From the north will Evil come
forth, upon all the inhabitants of the earth."*
                              (Bahir, 1979: para.162, p.60)

Scholem confirms this. The *Zohar* identifies evil with
sefira Geburah, "the quality of strict justice, rigor and judg-
ment in and by God, which is the fundamental cause of evil."
(Scholem, 1941: 237). The archangel Gabriel is associated with
Geburah; his name comes from Geburah-el.

For Rabbi Isaac Luria (1534–1572), leader of the last
great school of the Kabbalah, cosmic history is a process by
which God purifies Himself by getting rid of the evil in His
system (Scholem, 1969: 111). The deity concentrated his
destructive aggression in sefira number five, Geburah or
Mars, and then cut off the surplus. This surplus then became
the angry demons (Scholem, 1969: 112).

How can humans help God? By the process of *tikkun*
or harmonious correction. The problem with Zair Anpin, the
Impatient or Small Countenance, is that he is all masculine
and cut off from the feminine. His aggression is destructive
and out of control because he is cut off from his nurturing
feminine counterpart (Scholem, 1969: 114). The cosmic task is
to reintegrate masculine and feminine, aggression and nurturing, and achieve wholeness. This extraordinary analysis
anticipates the system of Jung, and is one of the historical high
points of human religious thought.

PRACTICE THREE

Thanks to the Hermetic axiom, "as above, so below,"
the sefirot of the Kabbalah are a diagram of the cosmos *and* a
diagram of the *microcosm*, namely, the human being. One of
the ways of using the Kabbalah is to analyze each sefira in

terms of the elements, make the appropriate color diagrams, and then use one these diagrams to do an inner journey and visit a particular sefira. In so doing, we are visiting a sector of our own structure in the inner planes, or a sector of the Jungian collective unconscious. The purpose of such a visit is self-knowledge. The vision we obtain will tell us how we are doing in a particular area of life.

The elements have standard symbols. Earth is a yellow square. Water is a silver crescent (tips up). Fire is a red triangle. Air is a blue circle. Ether is a purple oval in a vertical position. Whenever possible, the colors are bright primary colors. We also need to know some of the composites or combinations of elements:

1. Earth of Earth is a yellow square within a yellow square:

2. Water of Earth is a silver crescent within a yellow square:

3. Fire of Earth is a red triangle within a yellow square:

4. Air of Earth is a blue circle within a yellow square:

5. Water of Water is a silver crescent within a silver crescent:

6. Fire of Water is a red triangle within a silver crescent:

7. Air of Water is a blue circle within a silver crescent:

8. Water of Fire is a silver crescent within a red triangle:

9. Fire of Fire is a red triangle within a red triangle:

10. Air of Fire is a blue circle within a red triangle:

11. Water of Air is a silver crescent within
a blue circle:

12. Fire of Air is a red triangle within
a blue circle:

13. Air of Air is a blue circle within
a blue circle:

14. Air of Ether is a blue circle within
a purple oval:

As explained earlier, the right column of the sefirot (two, four, seven) is Water. The left column (three, five, eight) is Fire. And the middle column (one, Da'at, six, nine, ten) is Air. Horizontally, from the bottom up, sefira ten is in the Earth zone. Sefirot seven, eight, and nine are in the Water zone. Sefirot four, five, and six are in the Fire zone. Sefirot two, three, and Da'at are in the Air zone. Sefira one is in the Ether zone. This analysis yields the result shown in figure thirteen.

Notice that sefira number ten, or planet Earth, contains four combinations, and that these are organized as a polar arrangement with East-West (Fire-Water) inversion. This analysis is identical to the one given by Ophiel (Ophiel, 1972: 85) (Ophiel, 1976: 100–101).

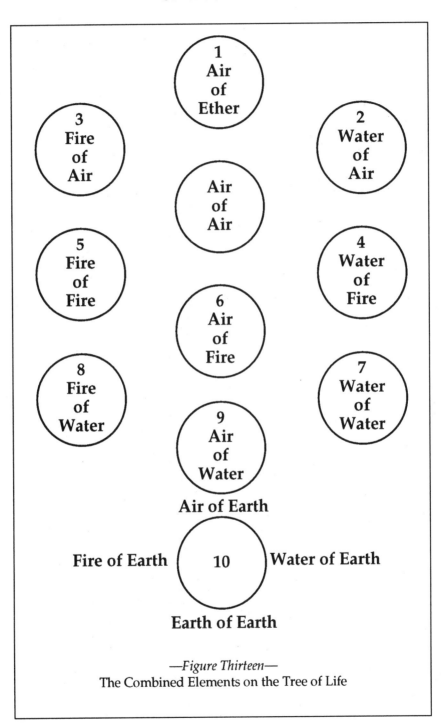

—*Figure Thirteen*—
The Combined Elements on the Tree of Life

The 14 diagrams of composite elements as shown above can be manufactured by purchasing glossy colored paper at an art supply store, and pasting it on sheets of cardboard.

Procedure

We are going to show you how to do *tattwa* journeys. *Tattwa* is the Hindu name for the elements. Tattwa journeys were a major activity of various members of the famous Hermetic Order of the Golden Dawn. However, we will add two items to their procedure: the company of your power animal, and a source of monotonous sonic input (to take you into the required altered state of consciousness). For a monotonous sonic input, try a musical sound device such as John Stannard's Energy Chime. It must be something that sits beside you on your desk, and something that you can strike with a stick or beater, with one hand, while you go on a journey.

You will use one card per journey. The composite element symbol on the card will be used as a doorway through which you can enter a sector of the inner planes. You will make this journey in the company of your power animal. When you return to the ordinary world, you will seal your doorway by drawing over it a banishing pentagram of white light. See figure fourteen.

—*Figure Fourteen*—
A Banishing Pentagram of White Light

Start at the top and follow the arrow. Make one continuous line of white light until you end up at the top (your point of departure). Then stab the center of the pentagram. This provides your doorway with a protective seal.

1. Sit at your desk, at night, with light from a lamp shining on your chosen card. Start striking your Energy Chime. Stare at the card and try not to blink. After a couple of minutes you will see that the diagram starts to shimmer.

2. Change to a blank (white) card. You should now be seeing your composite element symbol in its complementary colors.

3. Repeat steps 1 and 2 three times. On the fourth time, turn off the light and close your eyes. You should see your composite element symbol in strong complementary colors.

4. Call your power animal. Use your imagination to either enlarge the symbol or to reduce yourself in size. The composite symbol is a doorway. Enter that doorway together with your power animal. Remember to continue to strike your Energy Chime. At first you will see smoke or fog. Wait until it clears and try to see what kind of scene you have before you. Ask your power animal about the identity or meaning of what you see.

5. After you finish your visit, come out through your door way. If the colors are still complementary colors, then reverse them. Seal the doorway with a banishing pentagram of white light. Write down your journey.

You have just visited an area of yourself or a domain in your life. You may have visited your aggression and courage (sefira number five, or Fire of Fire), or you may have visited your originality and creativity (sefira number two or Water of Air), or you may have visited your capacity for love and nurturing (sefira number seven, or Water of Water). What did you find? How are you doing in that domain? Is that an area of life that needs more work?

Sample Tattwa Journey

One of us, George, who is an academic, visited sefira number eight, which is the rational intellect and competition:

The scene shows two rocky flatlands or mesas on top of a mountain. Reddish-brown rock. In between the two flat areas I see a sharp cleft, drop, or abyss from which purple light or fog rises. Beyond the edge of the two mesas I see light purple fog and clouds fading to white. The two flat areas of stone are linked by a flat stone bridge. On the bridge is a large bird, either a small eagle or an owl. It keeps changing between eagle and owl. The large bird faces left on the bridge. It has brown feathers and large yellow eyes. Beyond the edge of the two mesas the fog and clouds change to a tightly-packed herd of charging bulls. But the bulls are contained or held at bay.

Question to power animal: "What is that?"

Answer: "Bull is Bull."

Question to power animal: "What is the purple light or fog that comes up from the cleft?"

Answer: "The non-solid."

Question to power animal: "Anything else to learn here?"

Answer: "No."

So we exit the turquoise triangle inside a black crescent. We reverse the colors to a red triangle inside a silver crescent. We seal with a banishing pentagram of white light.

Interpretation:

The eagle on the bridge is the sharp, analytical, destructive intellect. It is turning into an owl, which is wisdom. It faces "left" because that is my political orientation. The two flat stone mesas are my two areas of intellectual interest: an academic area, and shamanism and ritual magic. The charging bulls in the clouds are the empty verbiage and double-talk that afflicts some academic areas and some new age discourse.

CHAPTER FOUR

THE
CHRISTIAN KABBALAH
AND THE TAROT

The Christian Kabbalah was in-
vented around 1486 C.E. by Giovanni Pico della Mirandola, a
Florentine aristocrat, philosopher, magician and humanist of
the Renaissance (Scholem, 1987: 197). Pico relied on Latin
translations of Hebrew texts (e.g., The *Bahir*, the writings of
Abraham Abulafia). These translations were prepared by
Flavius Mithridates, a Jewish convert to Christianity, who was
a teacher of oriental languages. Mithridates was convinced
that the Kabbalah pre-figured the Trinity, and that Hebrew
letter-number permutations (i.e, *gematria*) and substitutions
(i.e., *temurah*) proved that Jesus was indeed the Messiah. To
this end, he adulterated his translations with crucial and ten-
dentious interpolations (Wirszubski, 1989: 84–118). Pico believed that the Kabbalah proved the truth of Christianity. He
also believed in the unity of truth; so he combined Kabbalah
with Neoplatonism and the *Corpus Hermeticum*. In the latter,
his intuition was correct. The Jewish Gnosticism of the Kabbalah and the pagan Gnosticism of the *Hermetica* share an obvious common ground (Yates, 1969: 108). Johannes Reuchlin's

De Arte Cabalistica (1517 C.E.) expanded on Pico's conclusions. "Through Reuchlin, Pico's Cabalist magic leads straight on to the angel magic of Trithemius or of Cornelius Agrippa" (Yates, 1969: 102). When the dust settled, it turned out that the Christian Kabbalists had made certain drastic changes in the Jewish Kabbalah.

a. They reassigned the Hebrew letters to paths, seemingly at random, and with total disregard for the internal division of three mother letters, seven doubles, and 12 simple letters.

b. They gave new and arbitrary astrological attributions to the seven double letters:

Jewish Attributions		Christian Attributions	
Beth	— Saturn	Beth	— Mercury
Gimmel	— Jupiter	Gimmel	— Moon
Daleth	— Mars	Daleth	— Venus
Kaph	— Sun	Kaph	— Jupiter
Pe	— Venus	Pe	— Mars
Resh	— Mercury	Resh	— Sun
Tav	— Moon	Tav	— Saturn

—Figure Fifteen—
Astrological Attributions

c. They removed the path that had linked sefirot five and two, and the path that had linked sefirot four and three. They added two new paths at the bottom, linking sefirot ten and eight, and ten and seven.

These changes are so arbitrary and so drastic, that we conclude that *the paths have been hopelessly damaged and contaminated by incoherence, and that they have to be abandoned.* What we retain is the shamanic root of the Kabbalah, the common ground between the Jewish and the Christian Kabbalah, which belongs to neither faith: the magnificent Gnostic structure of the sefirot organized into the World Tree of shamanism.

In addition, the Christian Kabbalists gave the sefirot astrological attributions. The astrological planets are the Greco-Roman gods. These attributions are possible, because all pantheons contain psychological systems. For example, Geburah, or Power, can be recognized as aggression and identified with Mars. Furthermore, these attributions are legitimate, because they are nothing more than a return to the Gnostic identification of archons or powers with planetary spirits.

The Christian Kabbalah only used the seven astrological symbols known to antiquity. We suggest that Da'at is Neptune or mystical knowledge. Since sefira number three is Saturn, and therefore tradition, conservatism, and old age, we suggest that sefira number two is Uranus, the symbol of novelty, creativity, and originality. (Because the left and right columns or pillars of the Tree, represent polar opposites). Number one has some features of Pluto: all beginnings and endings.

In simple language, the astrological attributions and domains represented by the sefirot are as indicated in figure sixteen.

Notice how the force of destruction (number five) is continued in the aggressive intellect (number eight). Likewise, the force of growth (number four) is continued as love and nurturing (number seven). In a Jungian sense, aggression is male or an animus characteristic, and nurturing is female or an anima characteristic. The mother (number three) counterbalances the masculine aggressive left column, while the Father (number two) counterbalances the feminine nurturing right column.

ON THE TAROT

The Tarot trumps were probably invented in northern Italy, possibly in Ferrara, around 1440 C.E., as illustrations to

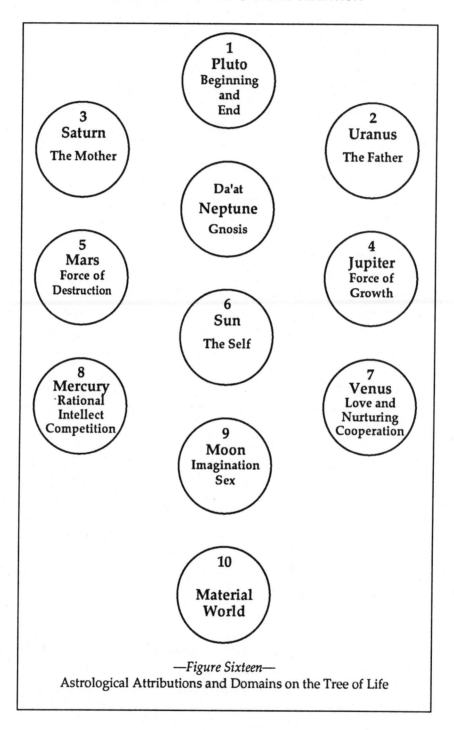

—*Figure Sixteen*—
Astrological Attributions and Domains on the Tree of Life

a cycle of poems or *Triumphs* by Petrarch. In 1956, Gertrude Moakley pointed out that the trumps tell the same story as the poems, and had the same name — *trionfi* (Shephard, 1985: 72). In 1463 C.E., in Florence, the humanist and magician Marcilio Ficino translated the pagan Gnostic *Corpus Hermeticum* (circa 2nd century C.E.) into Latin. This added impetus to astral mysticism, and the Tarot trumps were given astrological symbolism and structure. However, as reconstructed by John Shephard, these astrological attributions are radically different from those given to the Tarot trumps in the late 19th century by the Golden Dawn. See figure seventeen.

A common symbol shared between the Shephard and Golden Dawn attributions is found in five trumps (Empress, Emperor, Devil, Sun, World), and nothing in the remaining 17 trumps.

Following Eliphas Levi (Alphonse-Louis Constant), S. L. MacGregor Mathers, a founder of the Golden Dawn, identified the Tarot trumps with the Hebrew consonants, in alphabetical order, for the purpose of linking the 22 Tarot trumps with the paths of the Christian Kabbalah. In this identification, the seven double letters retained the astrological attributions which they had acquired in the Christian Kabbalah of the Renaissance.

How successful or coherent is this linkage? To compare the meanings of two sets of symbols requires that both sets have stable meanings. The Tarot trumps have a main tradition of stable meanings (although some modern decks change or set aside these meanings). The problem lies with the paths of the Christian Kabbalah, where 12—or more than half—are assigned to the Tropical zodiac.

The Tropical zodiac attempts to link two sets of entities:

a. Twelve constellations along the band of the ecliptic (the apparent path of the Sun around the Earth).

b. A classification of all human beings into 12 character types.

Because of the precession of the equinoxes, the Tropical signs

Trumps	Shephard	Golden Dawn	
Fool		Aleph	—Air
Magician	Moon in Cancer	Beth	—Mercury
High Priestess (Popess)	Mercury in Gemini	Gimmel	—Moon
Empress	Venus in Taurus	Daleth	—Venus
Emperor	Mars in Aries	He	—Aries
Hierophant (Pope)	Jupiter in Pisces	Vau	—Taurus
Lovers	Sun	Zain	—Gemini
Chariot	Sun in Leo	Heth	—Cancer
Strength (Fortitude)	Mars in Scorpio	Teth	—Leo
Hermit	Saturn in Aquarius	Yod	—Virgo
Wheel of Fortune	Venus in Libra	Kaph	—Jupiter
Justice	Mercury in Virgo	Lamed	—Libra
Hanged Man	Jupiter in Saggitarius	Mem	—Water
Death	Saturn in Capricorn	Nun	—Scorpio
Temperance	Moon	Samekh	—Saggitarius
Devil	Mars in Capricorn	Ayin	—Capricorn
Tower	Mercury in Virgo	Pe	—Mars
Star	Venus in Pisces	Tzaddi	—Aquarius
Moon	Moon in Taurus	Qoph	—Pisces
Sun	Sun in Aries	Resh	—Sun
Judgment	Jupiter in Cancer	Shin	—Fire
World (Universe)	Saturn in Libra	Tav	—Saturn

—*Figure Seventeen*—
Comparison of Astrological Attributions and the Tarot Trumps
(Shephard, 1985: 71; Regardie, 1984: vol. II, 8–9)

no longer correspond to the constellations. For example, most living persons said to be born with the Sun in Tropical Taurus were really born with the Sun in Aries.

The philosophy of science tells us that a successful classification must have categories that are logically mutually exclusive (no overlaps) and internally homogeneous. The extensive, disparate and often contradictory character traits listed under each Tropical Sun sign violate these criteria. It follows that the signs of the Tropical zodiac lack sufficiently stable or coherent meanings. We conclude that it is impossible to evaluate the alleged link between the meanings of the Tarot trumps and the meanings of the paths of the Christian Kabbalah.

The Christian Kabbalah has been around for 500 years. The attribution of Tarot trumps to Christian Kabbalah paths has been on the scene for 100 years. All of this means that the Christian Kabbalah exists in the inner planes as a fairly stable artificial elemental. An artificial elemental is a creation of its believers. The structure of this artificial elemental is reinforced by contemporary Christian occultists who engage in what they call *pathworking.* This is an inner journey which uses a Tarot trump as a doorway to gain access to a particular path. Pathworking is usually a group activity. Its success depends on expectations, your knowledge of Christian Kabbalah correspondences and your sympathy with Christian symbolism.

The Jewish Kabbalah is also an artificial elemental, but a much older and more coherent one. The Jewish Kabbalah and the Christian Kabbalah are culture-bound to the belief systems of their respective faiths. The archetypal reality behind both is the cross-cultural or trans-cultural symbol of the shamanic world tree.

PRACTICE FOUR

We are going to teach you how to use the Tarot trumps as doorways for visionary journeys. Select a standard Tarot deck which has vivid colors and much detail. The Aleister Crowley - Frieda Harris deck is very effective for this purpose. In addition, you will need a source of monotonous sonic input, such as a drumming tape. We prefer a musical sound device, such as John Stannard's Energy Chime, which can sit on a desk and be played manually. The procedure is as follows:

1. Sit comfortably at a desk with a good light, and examine the Tarot trump while listening to your source of monotonous sonic input. Try to memorize the visual details.

2. Close your eyes and turn off the light.

3. Imagine that the picture on the trump covers the entire surface of a door, and that this door is going to open toward you.

4. Call your power animal and ask it to accompany you through the open doorway. You may say something like, "Please take me through the open doorway to visit what lies beyond."

5. Together with your power animal, enter the domain beyond the doorway and describe what you see.

6. If you encounter fog, or smoke, or clouds, wait for it to settle and reveal a scene. If you encounter uniform darkness or uniform light, you can change this by chanting a Word of Power that works for you (e.g., EH - HEH - YEH or I - A - O [ee-ah-oh]). If in doubt, ask your power animal.

7. As scenes or events unfold, you can ask your power animal to interpret or explain.

8. When your visit is finished, you and your power animal exit through the doorway, close the door, and seal the closed door with a banishing pentagram.

What follows is an account of journeys into the 22 Tarot trumps of the Crowley deck, done by George, over a period of several weeks. The latest edition of the Crowley deck has three alternative trumps for the Magus.

Fool

A voice says "All Beginnings." Daylight, mid-morning. We are standing on a barren, off-white rock hill. Power animal says "Barren." Can we go to the top? "You will still find nothing."

Chant IAO. Scene changes to a green, well-kept lawn

and tree behind a wall and gate. Chant IAO. A purple mountain with astral blue energy on top. Power animal says "You can choose between barren freedom and fruitful but confined order." Choice between undesirable alternatives.

Magus One

Night and stars. We stand on land facing a black lake. Power animal says "This is death."

Chant IAO. In the distance, hills become outlined in light. Chant EH - HEH - YEH. An old wooden boat or small ship sails toward us. Something like fire burns inside. Is this a Viking funeral? I see a grotesque face carved on the prow. A tall, elderly male comes out of the ship and floats or glides toward us. He has curly hair, long beard, wears a robe, and is outlined in orange-yellow energy. Power animal says "A Magus."

"Who are you, sir?"

"Nodens."

"What do you have to teach me?"

"If you stepped into this poisonous water, you would die. The point is to float or glide over it. To traverse the poison of the world without being destroyed. Then you can go anywhere. That is freedom."

Chant IAO. A silver, upright pentagram appears over his face. He returns to the boat and leaves.

Magus Two

Green hills with grass. Several hundred sheep face away from us. Who are these? Power animal says "People."

Chant IAO. Blue mountains with huge boulders. A brilliant morning sun begins to rise. Chant EH - HEH - YEH. Fog over water. A rust colored boat comes out of the fog. It is almost flat like a canoe, with both ends up. Inside rests an adult figure, hooded and robed in black velvet. The figure rises and comes forward. I see two piercing eyes and a grey beard. Power animal says "A Magus."

"Who are you, sir?"

"Vox."

"What can you teach me?"

"This water is not poisoned. Death is the ultimate Magus, it transforms everything and everyone."

The figure leaves.

Magus Three

Green indoor pool. Faint illumination. An enormous shark rises from the green water and shows me his teeth and jaws. Chant IAO. Purple-grey megalithic stones on a hill. Early morning sunrise. A tall man in a white robe comes forth. He has long, blond, curly hair, grey beard and green eyes.

"Who are you, sir?"

"Vale. I am the Magus of the East."

His arms hold two torches which burst into flames. An earthquake crack splits the earth beneath his feet. Instantly he lowers the torch in his left hand and closes or heals the split. He places his left hand on my head and gives me energy. I thank him. He leaves.

Priestess

Night sky with millions of stars. A low hill with megalithic stones. The full Moon above. Scene changes to a crescent Moon in an indigo sky, above the last traces of sunset. On the sides, large stone cliffs. Scene changes to thin golden trumpets with attached banners in a fan-like formation. Behind them, a steep black mountain with a huge diamond on top. Scene changes to full Moon shining over a valley with human and animal bones. Power animal says, "The kingdom of the Moon. The Valley of rebirth of the spirit." Scene changes to blue-green ocean seen from the sky.

Empress

A green field with a fence of white skulls. Beyond it, barren brown earth and a light brown building with an archway. In front of the archway, a row of fruit trees. Power animal says, "In the midst of life is death; and in the midst of barren death, is life."

Chant IAO. Scene changes to ornate golden chalice encrusted with jewels, mostly rubies and garnets. Chant EH - HEH - YEH. Blue ocean with conical lavender mountains in the background.

Chant IAO. A stream of clear water flows down hill. Salmon swim against the current to reach their spawning ground and die. Power animal says, "Sex is an impersonal driving force at the service of reproduction. Humans are no different [than salmon]."

Hierophant

The Pope's head changes to a black crocodile. His hands change to black claws. Chant IAO. His head disappears and is replaced by the yellow light of an erupting volcano.

Chant IAO. A large metal trench with thousands of squirming white worms. An unpleasant odor. The worms are being processed and packaged. Power animal says, "This is organized hypocrisy."

Chant IAO. Standing statue of a dark, grey male appears on the right side.

"Who are you?"

"The drive for power."

Chant EH - HEH - YEH. A multitude of figures run or dance around a truncated pyramid. Power animal says, "The pyramid builders. This is a card of the misuse of spiritual power to dominate or subjugate other people."

Lovers

Mid-morning. We are standing on a brown-lavander flatland with many shallow pools. At intervals, the center of a pool will stir with large bubbles, indicating that it is an outlet for an underground hot spring. A few hundred feet in front of us a huge white geyser shoots up, then quiets down. What is this? Power animal says, "Water [emotion, feeling]. Choice between opposites: the sudden tall powerful jet against the many shallow pools."

Chant IAO. From the air we see a square oriented to the quarters, like a mandala, on light purple ground. In the middle, a thin but endless column of white water rises to the sky. Power animal says, "This is the water version of the World Tree." Chant EH - HEH - YEH. A flat basin or valley surrounded by golden peaks. A diagonal row of stone obelisks crosses the black earth from upper left to lower right. A diagonal river of molten red lava runs from upper right to lower left. Power animal says, "These are choices."

Chariot

A castle on top of a mountain of redish-brown rock. People are attempting the arduous climb to reach the castle. Chant IAO. We are standing inside a round stone cave facing an entrance with jagged edges. Power animal says, "This is being born with great effort." Chant EH - HEH - YEH. A sunken house with brown door and ivy. The door opens, and an elderly retired person comes out. Power animal says, "Peace and security after life-long struggle."

Justice (Adjustment)

Bare trees have shed their yellow leaves on both sides of a gravel path. At the end of the path we find an old white horse or mule. He has worked all his life and now — to the glue factory. No justice here. Vision of a shallow trench with dead bodies: a massacre. Power animal says "The secret of justice is that there is no justice."

Chant IAO. Brown slaves pull huge blocks of granite with white ropes. "There is no justice in human history. We stand naked like the trees, devoid of leaves, waiting for winter and death."

Chant IAO. A forest clearing in a temperate zone. Two knights in armor, on horseback, come in from the left and the right. They fight with lances and swords. The one on the right falls. The one on the left dismounts and beheads him. What is this? Power animal says, "This is what lies behind justice." Is this justice? Power animal says, "You are asking to return to the premise, where you had parity."

Hermit

Field of white poppy flowers. What is this? Power animal says, "Poppy is opium." What is the connection to the Hermit? "Flight from the pain of life."

Chant IAO. Two huge hills of coal separated by narrow red floor. What is this? Power animal says, "Coal is fuel that produces heat and energy. Meditation of the Hermit is a fuel. The inner as resource for the outer."

Chant EH - HEH - YEH. A brown horse with a green mane appears in middle-ground center and gallops toward us. The horse leaps over the path and stands before us. A tall, magnificent horse with black eyes. I touch its flank, near the neck, and feel muscle and strength. Power animal says, "This is silent endurance. He jumped over the path because it is a boundary." The path now shows smoke and small flames and turns into a fiery chasm.

Wheel of Fortune

It is night, and we are walking along a stone avenue. On the right is a row of megalithic tombs. Chant IAO. We are flying down a stone canyon. There is an orange - yellow glow from below. The chasm shows that the inside of the Earth is made of gold. I see streams of flowing molten gold. Power animal says, "The Earth is the wheel of fortune." Why the tombs at the beginning? "This is a place of desolation. The Earth is made of gold and is a place of desolation."

Chant EH - HEH - YEH. A winding highway at dusk. Many cars. I am a small animal that has just been run over and killed by a car. Power animal says, "The other side of fortune is misfortune."

Strength (Lust)

Clouds edged in blue and orange part to reveal two stone thrones. They face in opposite directions, sharing a common back. The stone is light brown with blue-green tri-angular designs. Power animal says, "Seats of the Gods. Opposites are united by having an area in common, and each attending to his or her own domain."

Chant IAO. Dark blue dawn. The mirror-like surface of a lake. Plants grow from the bottom. Brown and green flat leaves. I see a yellow and red lotus bloom. Power animal says, "The power of the feminine." Chant EH - HEH - YEH. A slender feminine figure in a light green robe with wide sleeves and beige cuffs, and delicate, long-fingered hands, spreads a silk table cloth on the grass of an island. She lays out dishes with food.

Chant IAO. Three angels, feet up, heads down, blow on golden trumpets. Below them, an orange flame appears. Power animal says, "The creation of life."

Hanged Man

We fly above the clouds. Below, I see dark brown crags and pastel fields outside a city. Power animal says, "Time to be above the battle."

Chant IAO. Golden fog clears to reveal the dark blue water of a lake or ocean. A human figure is drowning. A huge black crocodile-like monster comes up from the depths and swallows the drowning person. Power animal says, "The waters of death."

Chant IAO. North American Indian Sun Dance cere-mony. Muscular men, biceps pierced with leather straps, swing in a circle. Chant EH - HEH - YEH. A wreath of white flowers and green leaves trails a boat that carries a coffin. Someone pushes the coffin into the water.

Chant IAO. A human figure in dark blue robe and golden crown is burned at the stake.

Death

Flat, barren, lunar landscape. A black canyon in the foreground. A mile down, the fires of a thermonuclear furnace.

Chant IAO. Close-up of purple granite mountains.

Stretched horizontally are two dead snakes. What is this? Power animal says, "Not dead snakes, but the dead skin shed by snakes." Chant EH - HEH - YEH. A view from a military plane that is dropping bombs on a port city at night. Power animal says, "Technological death has no transcendence."

Chant IAO. A greenish terrain of flat polyhedrons. Ice floats in the North Pole? "Yes." The floor of death valley? "Yes." Scene changes to an underground crypt with smooth reddish columns. Power animal says, "The bones of generations."

Chant IAO. A very steep golden stairway. Power animal says, "The rest of you goes up." To the Upper World? "Yes."

Temperance (Art)

A pool amid round green hills. Two factors are producing concentric circles in the water: a dripping from above and bubbles from below. Power animal says, "Balance of above and below."

Chant IAO. A ship arrives and several small creatures climb on board. Power animal says, This is containment." Chant EH - HEH - YEH. Red diagonal lightning from the left. Blue diagonal lightning from the right. Both streams converge on a gold basin or container. [This is a Kabbalah arrangement: red Mars from left shoulder and blue Jupiter from right shoulder, converge on the golden heart center].

Devil

A thin, shallow stream in a dry river bed. In front and above, a huge Sun seen through fog. Power animal says, "Imbalance: too much fire and too little water." Chant EH - HEH - YEH. The whirling of a gigantic brown fan. From below, little human figures float up and are instantly destroyed. Power animal says, "Impersonal destruction."

Chant IAO. Exploding volcano. Molten lava. Huge, red-hot blocks blow up in every direction. Massive rivers of red lava. I see white human bones disintegrate in the lava flow. Power animal says, "Such waste."

Tower

Night. A river of glowing red lava falls like a waterfall and runs into a canyon. Four doves fly from left to right with olive branches in their beaks. Power animal says, "They are suing for peace because they have been overwhelmed."

Chant IAO. A tank rolls in from the right. It explodes, cracks in half, and its gun turret gets twisted. Power animal says, "Eventually, the Earth and its forces win over the efforts of man." Chant EH - HEH - YEH. A Roman galley, run by galley slaves, sails on a sea by a coast.

Star

Green lawn. Hot pink roses on the right. Exotic green cacti on the left. Power animal says, "Life force and beauty."

Chant IAO. Human hands open an old metal chest. It contains written documents. Power animal says, "Recovery of ancient knowledge." A light colored building with many windows, threatened by a blue ocean. Superimposed, the Potala palace of Tibet. Power animal says, "Center of wisdom." Chant EH - HEH - YEH. Rushes by a river bank. An abandoned baby. The baby grows up into a strong young man. Power animal says, "That which was lost or abandoned, recovers and develops."

Moon

Dawn. In a dark foreground, dogs and jackals are eating human corpses. Power animal says, "Humans get too upset over death. It is natural. The jackals might as well benefit."

Chant IAO. Empty plain with two black towers. Beyond them is a desert rock formed into an arch. Inside the arch, the full Moon in a blue sky. Peaceful. Chant EH - HEH - YEH. At eye level, a wave with small ripples moves forward on the wet sand. The ocean deposits the corpses of countless marine creatures on the sand. Power animal says, "All life began in the ocean."

Sun

Green fields, blue stream, the red tile roofs of an Italian city: a view of Florence in the Renaissance. Vertical flames, someone is being burned at the stake.

Chant IAO. A forest fire at night. Red-gold flames on the horizon are moving toward us. Next morning, under sunlight and fog, the smoky, charred remains of a forest.

Chant IAO. The left hand of a gold statue, palm up. Inside the palm, a human eye made of precious metals. Power animal says, "You pluck the eye to believe, and yet you need the eye to appreciate all this." Chant EH - HEH - YEH. From outer space, we watch a huge Sun rise behind the Earth. The Earth looks covered by blue ocean and lavender clouds.

Chant IAO. We fly over a huge blue-white waterfall coming from purple granite cliffs. Small boats with humans, paddling frantically, make the successful transit without capsizing. Power animal says, "Success in navigating the rapids and obstacles of life."

Judgment (Aeon)

Fog over land ravaged by fire. A brown, ornate, antique bookshelf holds a huge golden book. Power animal says, "The rebirth of knowledge after the fog of dogmatic ignorance."

Chant IAO. A very phallic mosque on the edge of the sea. Power animal says, "That too is rebirth." Green shoots reappear amid the blackened land. Chant EH - HEH - YEH. Fog clears to reveal an ocean with submerged and drowned cities. Power animal says, "Atlantis happens again and again. Notice that the temples of the old religion are gone." In the submerged buildings I recognize a Christian church, an Islamic mosque, and a Hebrew synagogue.

Chant IAO. Large angelic figures with gold wings fly on a horizontal plane above us. They are definitely non-human. Their golden faces have no expression. Power animal says, "The inner planes escape the catastrophe." Chant EH - HEH - YEH. A stone stairway on top of a large building. A priest in red appears. He wears a red mask over his eyes. He opens his arms. I feel the pull toward him. I look down and realize that this is a Maya temple pyramid. The priest wants me to come so that he can sacrifice me. Power animal says, "Those who succumb to the pull of dogmatic faiths end up sacrificed and gutted."

World (Universe)

We are standing in a warm, shallow stream. In front of us is a lush tropical forest. We see a plethora of animals: fish in the stream, a spotted leopard in the tall grass, a monkey swinging from a tree, a large snake.

Chant IAO. A golden bird leg ending in a golden claw holds black chains that are the spokes of a dark brown wheel. Power animal says, "The Wheel of cosmic destiny." Who is this being? Power animal says, "The claw is an aggressive weapon. The golden leg belongs to the alien, non-human reality at the center of our cosmos." [The Gnostic Abraxas!] Chant EH - HEH - YEH. Night on the edge between forest and savanna. Small, black human figures come down from the trees and hide in the tall grass together with their crude weapons. They begin to fan out. They are hunting. Fear and aggression. Human history begins.

Chant IAO. We are on a balcony, next to a railing, on the Potala of Tibet. Sunlight and very cold. Power animal says, "Top of the world."

A lama says to me: "Our oracles consult the Earth."

These journeys into the Tarot trumps are only an example of one set of visionary experiences obtained by one person, and ultimately meaningful and valid only for that person. We encourage the reader to use the Tarot trumps to obtain his or her own unique set of visionary experiences.

CHAPTER FIVE

A SUGGESTED
COSMOLOGY

We offer two cosmologies: a minimalist, agnostic version, and a shamanic and Gnostic version. The advantage of the former is that it allows the reader to detach from all symbolic systems and concentrate on the pragmatics of shamanism and magic. The advantage of the latter is that it plunges you into the very heart of the tradition.

MINIMALIST VERSION

1. Techniques that induce altered states of consciousness, particularly those based on monotonous sonic input, give us access to the alternate reality.

2. The alternate reality contains knowledge and shamanic or magical power.

3. If used within an ethical framework, this knowledge and power can be used to enhance individual and group survival, enrich life, increase gratification and promote personal growth.

SHAMANIC - GNOSTIC VERSION

After centuries of persecution and disguise, a coherent world view emerges at the center of the esoteric tradition. Not surprisingly, it is shamanic and Gnostic. We focus on the common ground of Witchcraft and ritual magic, after the latter has discarded the protective disguise of a Judeo-Christian format. We posit a primal Ultimate, but it is impersonal, so the infantilism of prayer becomes pointless. The Ultimate is what the covens call "the Void," what the Taoists call "the Tao," what the Kabbalists call the "Ain" or Nothingness and what Tibetan Buddhists call "the union of Emptiness and Bliss." The Ultimate or Void is not a person and is not concerned with our sex lives, our mistakes or even with our massacres. Nobody is looking after the fate of the bulk of humanity, as the victims of the Holocaust discovered the hard way. Likewise, nobody seems to be looking after the fate of plant life or animal life, currently threatened with extermination by the uncontrolled reproduction of a super-aggressive human species. At most one could say that if someone or something is monitoring the evolutionary process, then it or they are particularly indifferent to waste, suffering, torture, massacres and injustice.

While we find no evidence of ethical norms in Darwinian nature or in the objective cosmos, most world-wide shamanism recognized the need to pattern behavior within an ethical framework:

> *The shamans have played an essential role in the defense of the psychic integrity of the community. They are pre-eminently the antidemonic champions; they combat not only demons and disease, but also the black magicians ... In a general way, it can be said that shamanism defends life, health, fertility [and] the world of "light," against death, diseases, sterility, disaster and the world of "darkness" ... What is fundamental and universal is the shaman's struggle against what we could call "the powers of evil."*
>
> Eliade, 1964: 508–509

Ethical systems seem to involve something akin to what has been called the "Golden Rule" or positive reciprocity (e.g., "Love thy neighbor as thyself," or "Act as if your soul inhabited the bodies of your brothers," etc.). Here, the fundamental difference is one of range: who is your neighbor or who are your brothers? Some cultures limit the range to the kin group or to the tribe. Others extend the range to include the people of the nation or the civilization. Still others extend the range beyond all humans and include animals.

The religions of the father restrict spirit or soul to humans, and deny it to animals and plants. Buddhism denies ego identity, but recognizes spirit in all living beings. The animism which is historically associated with shamanism goes one step further and suggests that all which exists is alive. Animals and plants are fundamentally no different from humans and are equally deserving of dignity and respect. An adequate ethical system must include all sentient beings.

The spirit which is present in all sentient beings is in the form of sparks or fragments from the primal Ultimate or Void. These sparks or fragments are subject to periods of experience, stress, and suffering called "life." These periods are mediated by death and reincarnation. The latter is an automatic process, the cumulative effect of thousands of artificial elementals (of passion, rage, desire, thought and feeling) which we create every day, while awake or asleep. No one is punishing you. If punishment exists, then you punish yourself.

The gods and goddesses worshiped by humanity are artificial elementals created and fed by the thoughts and emotions of their believers. However, these artificial elementals are created on a basis of reality: the archetypes of the collective unconscious. Real gods and goddesses that are not human creations do exist, but they are neither all-knowing nor all-powerful. The real gods and goddesses are refined beings who were once human and are now far ahead of humanity. As anthropologist Peter Furst suggests, the gods are ancient shamans who went to the Upper World (Furst, 1977:

16). Likewise, it is probable that real demons exist but have nothing to do with the artificial elemental called Satan. In a sense, demons are primitive beings evolving on their own plane, in the Lower Astral. A human who contacts a demon is like someone who opens a cage with a hungry tiger. The hu-man, who should have more sense, is alone to blame for whatever nastiness ensues.

The Upper World is Yang: more male, active, expansive, abstract and intellectual. Its colors are more pastel and its smells more floral. The Lower World is Yin: more female, passive, concentrated, concrete and focused on feeling. Its colors are deeper and more primary and its smells are earthy. Upper World and Lower World exist vibrationally as more Yang or more Yin. Information and experiences exist at different vibrational levels. For example, if your question is about health or what plant will grow best in your garden, and you journey to the Upper World, the journey will end up in the Lower World where such information is accessible. If your question is concerned with the meaning of life, that information is accessible in the Upper World. We conclude that Upper World and Lower World are complementary and equally valuable and safe for human beings.

Evil exists in the Lower Astral. But the Lower Astral is only a part of the Middle World. In addition to the Lower Astral, the Middle World contains the record of past lives, the first stage on the journey of the recently dead and an inner plane counterpart to ordinary reality. For example, a journey to locate a lost item would be a journey into this counterpart in the Middle World.

If this account is roughly correct, then the age-long magical activity of invocation is questionable. No authentic god or goddess is likely to allow himself or herself to be brought down into a human body. If successful, invocation only brings in an artificial elemental (perhaps one of the historical gods or goddesses). The result is likely to be delusion. In experiential shamanism, it is axiomatic that we never call teachers or deities from the Upper World to come to us. Instead, *we go up to them.* There is only one exception to this rule. The energy known as the Cone of Power can be effectively invoked from the Void. Likewise, the energies that guard the cardinal points of the ritual circle, whether personified as Watchtowers, elemental king, or shamanic power animals, are properly invoked from the Void.

Invocation is a vertical procedure, since a human magician is trying to persuade a god or goddess to come down to his or her level. By way of contrast, evocation is a horizontal procedure. The magician is creating an artificial elemental to obtain knowledge or to produce a change in ordinary reality. Alternatively, the magician is trying to contact and communicate with beings in another, parallel domain or universe. These entities can be conceptualized as what Jung called semi-autonomous complexes of the collective unconscious. However, a perusal of written accounts (e.g., Bardon, 1975) reveals that most evocation is evocation of Middle World or Lower Astral entities. Obviously, this is unfortunate. It is as if the Western occult tradition has forgotten about the existence of the Lower World and its marvelous power animals. Yet, the fact remains, that the only safe and constructive evocation is evocation of power animals.

The passive activity of mediumship or channeling is even more questionable. The entranced medium or channel is like someone who unlocks his house and invites anyone to come in. Such visitors will be confused or destructive entities from the Middle World or Lower Astral, or the unhappy spirits of dead humans who are trapped or earthbound. The obvious danger to the medium or channel is possession. The worthlessness of this activity can be verified by examining the content of the communications received by most channels. No new knowledge is provided, and most of the messages are banal. From the viewpoint of shamanism, mediumship or channeling is an aberrant activity.

...unlike the shaman, the ... medium cannot control his [spirit] and is at its mercy or at that of any other dead person who wishes

*to "possess" him .... mediums, and "possessed" persons ... repre-
sent the aberrant shamanic tradition.*

                     Eliade, 1964: 347, 450

    We are interested in ways of access to altered states of
consciousness because these are the means for journeying,
visionary experience, and obtaining shamanic or magical
power. We seek visionary experience because it provides
knowledge and wisdom. We seek shamanic or magical power
because it gives us power over our own lives. It enables us to
help ourselves and to help others. This is the only legitimate
use of power. Attempts to control others are not only unethical, but ultimately futile. Shamanic or magical power exists
for the purpose of handling *this* life. It gives us an edge or
small advantage in precisely those areas where, regardless of
wealth or worldly power, humans are at the mercy of fate. In
addition, the euphoria of shamanic practice is a natural antidote to depression and to the stress of living in an industrial
society.

    From the paleolithic era through the recent 6,000 years
of history, various non-drug, non-hallucinogenic techniques
for obtaining altered states of consciousness have been discovered or developed. One way of listing these techniques is
by examining their association with the various senses and
with the elements. Earth is associated with smell, and Water
is associated with taste: here belongs the technique of fasting.
Fire is associated with sight: here belong procedures that use
lights, darkness, and colors, such as the tattwa cards with colored symbols of compound elements which we used to visit
the sefirot. Air is associated with touch and the kinesthetic
sense. Here belong shamanic dancing, the whirling of Sufi
dervishes and the whirling dances of the covens, and certain
body postures that induce trance, such as the shaman squat
(you squat on the floor with hands holding ankles and head
on knees). There is evidence that Jewish Merkabah mystics
made use of the shaman squat, plus singing ecstatic hymns,
to induce visions (Scholem, 1987: 15). Aether, the fifth ele-

ment, is associated with sound. Here belong shamanic drumming, shamanic rattling, the Didjeridu of the Australian aborigines, shamanic power songs, whistling, the chanting of mantras, and the vibration of Words of Power.

Words of Power are a particular contribution of the Western magical tradition. Words of Power range all the way from one-syllable terms to the lengthy and barbaric formulas of John Dee's Enochian. Actually, any one to four-syllable word will do, provided that it is from an alien language and that you can vibrate it. It is a matter of trial and error. Many of the Hebrew names of the deity used by the Golden Dawn do not vibrate, and are useless as Words of Power. Try chanting the Gnostic IAO (eee - ah - oh), starting as far back in the throat as possible. Then try the Hindu AUM (Ah - uh - mm), starting far back in the throat, with the mouth open, and finishing with closed lips. Now try the Hebrew EH - HEH - YEH. When the vibration occurs, you will know it. To successfully vibrate a word of power, you must do it with your entire body, mind, and spirit. Aleister Crowley recommends that you start by vibrating the word in your entire body (Michaelsen, 1989 : 15). Then try focusing the sound vibration at a point a few inches above your head or at your feet. Chanting Words of Power is a very effective device for reaching an altered state of consciousness. Another intriguing possibility is to enter the shamanic trance with the aid of monotonous sonic input, and ask your power animal to give you one or more Words of Power. There is reason to expect that any Words of Power obtained directly from your own unconscious will work for you alone, and be particularly effective.

Another way of classifying methods for inducing altered states of consciousness is to contrast those that quiet down or inhibit with those that excite. Here, monotonous sonic input figures in both columns because it can be used while sitting quietly and meditating, or while dancing and rattling. See figure eighteen.

This table is a modified version of the one presented by magician Peter J. Carroll (Carroll, 1987: 33). The point of

Inhibitory Mode	Excitatory Mode
Meditation Body postures	Drumming, dancing, rattling, chanting
Slow breathing	Fast breathing
Hypnosis	Shamanic Walk
Fasting	Sex
Sensory Deprivation	Sensory Overload

—*Figure Eighteen*—
Comparison of Inhibatory and Excitatory Modes of
Altered States of Consciousness

this table is that you can use either inhibitory or excitatory methods, but not both in combination or at the same time. By meditation we mean the Eastern methods (Hindu, Taoist, Buddhist) which discipline the mind to shut off the internal dialogue. Slow breathing is a well-known Yogic technique that does the same thing. Fast breathing or hyperventilation is used by the Rebirthing movement and in the workshops of Stanislav Grof. The shamanic walk is walking while looking at the horizon with eyes unfocused, and giving your complete attention to visual input (Carroll, 1987: 34; Castaneda, 1974: 21). It eventually shuts off the internal dialogue. Motionless body postures include the shaman squat and other trance inducing postures. They are currently being investigated by Felicitas Goodman (Goodman, 1988: 53-61). The use of sex for magical purposes will be described later on.

Still another way of examining procedures for inducing the shamanic state of consciousness is to view altered

states of consciousness in terms of their physiological corre-
lates. Cortical arousal (see figure nineteen) is measured by
the Electroencephalograph (EEG) and body arousal is measured by Electrical Skin Resistance (ESR). Hypnosis is associated with low body arousal (relaxation) but not with any
particular changes in EEG (Tart, 1972: 499; Cade and Coxhead, 1989: 31). Also, hypnosis seems to involve dissociation
and regression. Zen meditation and Yogi meditation (to a
level of *samadhi*), which require a relaxed and motionless
body, are associated with low body arousal and low cortical
arousal or EEG in the alpha - theta - delta range (Cade and
Coxhead, 1989: 168, 172-173). Transcendental Meditation or
TM, which uses mantras, is also associated with low body
arousal and low cortical arousal or EEG in the alpha - theta-
delta range (Cade and Coxhead, 1989: 169-170).

Mediumship or channeling is a dissociated state which
is correlated with *high* body arousal and low cortical arousal
or EEG in the alpha - theta - delta range (Cade and Coxhead,
1989: 150-151). Shamanic Consciousness is also a dissociated
state which seems to be correlated with *high* body arousal
(Cade and Coxhead, 1989: 38, 94), and low cortical arousal or
EEG in the alpha - theta - delta range (Goodman, 1988: 10). Nevertheless, phenomenologically, mediumship and shamanic
consciousness are radically different, because, as we stated
earlier, shamanic consciousness is *not* possession. Furthermore,
shamanic consciousness is associated more with hunter -
gatherer societies, while mediumship or possession is associated with agricultural societies (Goodman, 1988: 42, 47-48).

Meditation and shamanic consciousness are not identical. Here is a discussion of how various shamanic techniques
induce and sustain the shamanic state of consciousness:

Shamanic Dancing:

    a. The sound of rattle and/or drum moves consciousness
       to the alpha - theta range;

    b. Dancing keeps body arousal high.

Cortical Arousal (EEG)			
		High Beta	Low Alpha-Theta-Delta
Body Arousal (ESR)	High	Ordinary waking Consciousness	Shamanic Consciousness Mediumship or Possession
	Low		Zen Meditation Yogi Meditation TM Meditation

—*Figure Nineteen*—
(Adapted from Cade and Coxhead, 1989: 42)

Shaman's Walk:

    a. Eyes out of focus, and the ensuing state of no thought, moves consciousness to the alpha - theta range;

    b. Walking keeps body arousal high.

Trance Dance of the !Kung Bushmen:

In the trance dance of the !Kung Bushmen we find the same principles at work. The singing of the women provides the monotonous sonic input that shifts consciousness to the alpha - theta range while the dance of the men keeps their body in high arousal.

The Tibetan 108,000 Vajrayana Prostrations:

    a. Standing with hands over head, the practitioner lays

down completely so that forehead, chest, and knees touch the ground. This repeated exercise maintains high body arousal.

b. At the same time, the practitioner engages in an elaborate visualization of the meditation Buddhas. This takes consciousness into the alpha - theta range (Lewis in Monrreale, 1988: 204).

Michael Harner's Technique of Simultaneous Narration:

a. The sound of the drum takes consciousness into the alpha - theta - delta range.

b. Narrating the journey out loud, as it happens, keeps body arousal high.

In summary, a successful shamanic technique involves two procedures or activities: the first (e.g., walking, singing, dancing, talking) keeps the body in high arousal, while the second (monotonous sonic input), moves consciousness into the alpha - theta - delta range.

THE ENERGY CENTERS

The Western occult tradition recognizes the Hindu chakras or energy vortices located along the spine in the etheric body. Any competent psychic or clairvoyant can see them and verify which are open, closed, rotating, and so forth. The Western tradition suggests that the best and safest way to develop the chakras and arouse their energy is to work on them indirectly, from the astral, using the creative imagination. For this purpose, we need another diagram of the sefirot on the Tree as shown in figure twenty.

The brilliant white sphere (number one) is above your head. The grey-gold sphere (number two) is in the air, adjacent to your right ear. The black sphere (number three) is in the air, adjacent to your left ear. The purple sphere is on your

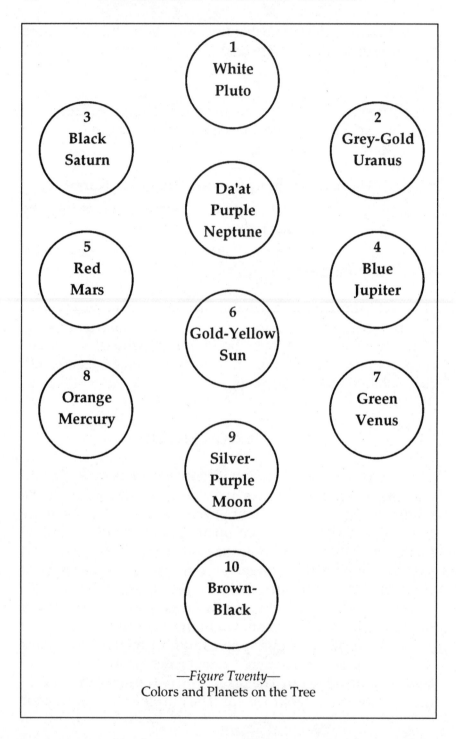

—*Figure Twenty*—
Colors and Planets on the Tree

lower throat. The sphere of primary blue (number four) is on your right shoulder. The sphere of primary red (number five) is on your left shoulder. The gold-yellow sphere (number six) is on your heart. The green sphere (number seven) is on your right hip. The orange sphere (number eight) is on your left hip. The sphere with silver and flecks of purple (number nine) is on your genitals. The brown-black sphere (number ten) begins at your ankles and extends below your feet. You are standing on it. Your creative imagination can be used to imprint the Tree of the sefirot in your aura for the purpose of developing magical power.

PRACTICE FIVE

We are going to teach you two versions of the famous Middle Pillar exercise. The technique gets its name from the middle column of sefirot (numbers one, Da'at, six, nine, and ten). The simple version here is our version of the one which was transmitted, rediscovered, or invented by the Hermetic Order of the Golden Dawn. Its purpose is to awaken the magical centers so as to develop the ability to do ritual magic (Regardie, 1984: Vol. VI, 27). Without this energy, a magical ritual remains dead, without power, nothing more than a piece of dramaturgy that brings no results. You will have to do the Middle Pillar exercise on a regular basis, for several months, before you begin to feel the energy. Some people see the energy, others perceive it by touch or kinesthetically.

In addition, we are going to teach you a more complex version of the Middle Pillar, one that uses all the sefirot. We have developed this complex version, and verified its greater effectiveness, through clairvoyant means. We recommend that you begin by learning and practicing the simple version, until it becomes easy and automatic. Only then do you move on to the complex version.

The Simple Version:

Stand facing North, with your hands above your head, making the sign of the pyramid. The sign of the pyramid involves joining your two index fingers so as to make a sharp angle, touching your thumbs, and folding the other fingers. Visualize a brilliant sphere of white light pulsating a few inches above your head. Vibrate out loud the Word of Power EH - HEH - YEH several times, focusing the sound vibration in the sphere of white light. EH - HEH - YEH is a Hebrew name of the deity which is quite effective. If that does not work for you, then try another Word of Power, such as IAO (eee - ah - oh).

Lower your arms. Visualize a ray of white light piercing your head and activating the purple sphere on your throat. Vibrate your Word of Power several times, focusing the sound on the purple sphere. Visualize a ray of white light from the purple sphere moving down and activating the golden sphere on your heart. Vibrate your Word of Power several times, focusing the sound on the golden sphere. Visualize a ray of white light from the golden sphere moving down and activating the silver-purple sphere on your genitals. Vibrate your Word of Power several times, focusing the sound on the silver-purple sphere. Visualize a ray of white light from the silver-purple sphere moving down and activating the brown-black sphere at your feet. Vibrate your Word of Power several times, focusing the sound on the brown-black sphere.

Now the brown-black sphere changes to a sphere of brilliant white light. Continue to vibrate your Word of Power. Follow the light back up to the silver-purple sphere which turns brilliant white. Vibrate your Word of Power several times on this brilliant white sphere. Follow the light up to the golden sphere which turns brilliant white. Vibrate your Word of Power several times on this brilliant white sphere. Follow the light up to the purple sphere which turns brilliant white. Vibrate your Word of Power several times on this brilliant white sphere. Follow the light up to the brilliant white sphere above your head. Vibrate your Word of Power several times on this brilliant white sphere.

What follows is known as *Circulation of the Body of Light* and is an essential part of this procedure:

1. Inhale. As you exhale slowly, visualize a cascade of white light pouring from the top sphere, down your left side, to your feet. Pause. As you inhale, visualize a thick wave of white light moving up your right side to the sphere at the top of your head. Pause. Repeat six times. Ideally, inhaling - pause - exhaling - pause, should be to the count of 4 - 2 - 4 - 2, or 6 - 3 - 6 - 3. You can synchronize this count to your pulse or heartbeat.

2. Inhale. As you exhale slowly, visualize a cascade of white light from the top sphere falling down your face and front of your body, down to your feet. Pause. As you inhale, visualize a thick wave of white light moving up your back to the top sphere. Pause. Repeat six times.

3. Go up on your toes, raise your arms to the top of your head, inhale slowly, and at the same time, visualize a jet of white light from the bottom sphere at your feet, piercing your body and rejoining the sphere above your head. Exhale slowly as you lower your arms, go down on your toes, and visualize that the light from the top sphere cascades around you in a Roman candle effect. Repeat six times.

You have done the simple version of the Middle Pillar exercise, and circulated the light to balance the energy throughout your aura. Patient repetition of this exercise for several months will eventually develop your ability to invoke the Watchtowers, invoke the Cone of Power, and do ritual magic.

The Complex Version:
Here you are going to visualize *all* the sefirot, activate them by vibrating your Word of Power, and visualize the link between them as a blue-silver cord. The *descending* sequence, which activates the sefirot in color, will go according to the following order: one, Da'at, three, two, six, five, four, nine, eight, seven, ten. The *ascending* sequence, in which the sefirot

turn to brilliant white light, will go according to the following order: ten, seven, eight, nine, four, five, six, two, three, Da'at, one. These sequences are not arbitrary. For example, if you examine the descending sequence, you will find that in each horizontal zone, we go from Air to Fire to Water.

1. Make the sign of the pyramid above your head, with both hands. Visualize a brilliant white or magnesium sphere (number one) above your head. Vibrate EH - HEH - YEH several times.

2. Bring the energy to the throat (Da'at). Visualize a purple sphere. Vibrate EH - HEH - YEH several times.

3. Bring the energy to the side of your left ear (number three). Visualize a black sphere. Vibrate EH - HEH - YEH several times.

4. Bring the energy over the head to the side of your right ear. Visualize a grey sphere with bits of gold (number two). Vibrate EH - HEH - YEH several times.

5. Bring the energy to the chest, over the heart (number six). Visualize a gold sphere. Vibrate EH - HEH - YEH several times.

6. Bring the energy to your left shoulder, and visualize a red sphere (number five). Vibrate EH - HEH - YEH several times.

7. Bring the energy to your right shoulder, and visualize a blue sphere (number four). Vibrate EH - HEH - YEH several times.

8. Bring the energy to your genitals, and visualize a silver sphere with bits of purple (number nine). Vibrate EH - HEH - YEH several times.

9. Bring the energy to your left hip, and visualize an orange sphere (number eight). Vibrate EH - HEH - YEH several times.

10. Bring the energy to your right hip, and visualize a green sphere (number seven). Vibrate EH - HEH - YEH several times.

11. Bring the energy to your feet, and visualize a brown-black sphere (number 10). Vibrate EH - HEH - YEH several times.

12. As you vibrate your Word of Power, the brown-black sphere changes into a sphere of brilliant white light.

13. Bring the energy to the green sphere on your right hip and visualize that it turns into a sphere of brilliant white light. Vibrate EH - HEH - YEH several times.

14. Bring the energy to the orange sphere on your left hip and visualize that it turns into a sphere of brilliant white light. Vibrate EH - HEH - YEH several times.

15. Bring the energy to the silver - purple sphere on your genitals and visualize that it turns into a sphere of brilliant white light. Vibrate EH - HEH - YEH several times.

16. Continue changing all spheres into brilliant white light and vibrating EH - HEH - YEH all the way back to the sphere above your head (number one)

17. Follow with Circulation of the Body of Light.

CHAPTER SIX

ON
MAGIC

Magic is the deliberate production of synchronistic effects. You carry out a subjective, inner-world operation or ritual in an altered state of consciousness and this operation or ritual produces a desired outcome or result in the objective, external world. We begin with a causal sequence that starts in the conscious psyche, *goes through the inner planes*, and produces an effect in the external domain. In other words, we use consciousness to program the collective unconscious, and somehow this produces a specific desired change in the objective material world. Of course, we don't know how a causal sequence in the inner planes can produce an effect in the external world. But the occult tradition affirms that this is precisely what happens. Furthermore, our own experience eventually confirms that the expected external event or condition does occur.

Strangely enough, in their private practice, Jungian analysts encounter the core phenomenon of magic: the fact that in an altered state of consciousness a subjective inner event can produce a change in the external world. Carl Jung borrowed the technique of inner journeys from the occult tradition and he named it "active imagination." Aside from dream interpretation, Jungian analysts are likely to have their analysands engage in active imagination. The analysand is asked to imagine a cave and a tunnel on the side of a mountain, and to walk in and establish sensory awareness. The tunnel extends horizontally into the mountain, and *then goes up.* The analysand finds an exit, describes the scene, and obtains a guide in human form. Together with the guide, the analysand can visit a problem area of the psyche (e.g., anger, fear, a dead father, an archetype). Jungians consider active imagination to be a journey into the collective unconscious. Analysands are cautioned against using active imagination to contact any known living person *because this will produce uncontrolled synchronicities.* As Jungian theorist Marie-Louise von Franz says,

> *You try honestly to overcome your affect in active imagination, things turn out well for you, and the other person who has annoyed you gets it back through a synchronistic event ... We have experienced that if done with living people the other person is affected, though we cannot explain how it works.*
>
> Von Franz, 1974: 184, 76

In our terms, Jungian active imagination is a journey into the lower levels of the shamanic Upper World. In its context, a subjective event produces an objective change, and the analyst "cannot explain how it works."

The reality of magic suggests the existence of a vast parallelism between the collective unconscious and the external physical world. Nevertheless, at this stage of our knowledge the pragmatic criterion alone is relevant. We do magic because we know that it works. We know this because we keep a written record or magical diary of every magical operation. We also record the occurrence of the specific and desired final outcome, if, when and how it happens. Such a written record is essential for reality-testing and as a means of avoiding self-delusion.

Regardless of wealth, power, science, and technology, every human life faces an irreducible margin of events and circumstances which are completely beyond our ordinary capacity or ability to predict or control. In addition, in many cases the exhaustive use of ordinary means only increases the probability of an outcome, without insuring it. This is the proper context in which to do magic. You do your utmost, using all available ordinary means, and then you add magic to tip the balance in your favor.

The successful practice of magic requires that we be able to focus the magical will. The magical will is *not* will power, it is *not* forcing yourself to do something or not do something against your impulses, wishes and drives. *The magical will is unity of desire* (Carroll, 1987: 55-56). In other words, your body and your psyche, your entire being, must want a *single,* specific effect, outcome, condition or change. Unresolved inner conflicts, or a shopping list of desired effects, shatter unity of desire and the attempt fails.

SOLITARY VERSUS GROUP PRACTICE

On the next point, George and Angelique disagree, so we give the reader two versions:

George's View:
Magic is an *intimate* activity; and this alone, aside from persecution, associates it with *solitude* and *secrecy.* Because the operation depends on mobilization of the magical will or unity of desire, it is easiest for the magician to operate alone. Here the drawback is the *lack of male-female polarity.* If two or more people try to do magic, then they must share *psychological intimacy.* Lack of this reduces the operation to play acting. Onlookers damage the intimacy and destroy the operation. Because of this, magic cannot be demonstrated to outsiders. Psychological intimacy is impossible for a group larger than a few people and difficult beyond two people. In practical

terms, and under ordinary circumstances, the larger the group, the weaker and more ineffectual the magical energy. However, under extraordinary circumstances — such as a lethal threat to the community from a plague or a ruthless enemy — hundreds or even thousands of persons could achieve a single focus of their magical will, with great effectiveness.

Angelique's View:

I agree that magic is best done by a male and female who share psychological intimacy. However, let us say that you have a well-trained group of 15 persons, and that this group has been working together harmoniously for some time. If these 15 people have *exactly the same intention*, then they can focus the magical will or achieve unity of desire. This is not only possible, but very effective, and much more powerful than magic done by a single person. Remember that the British covens successfully focused the magical will of hundreds to help stop the Nazi invasion during World War II.

The practice of magic involves bringing something into your life or the life of someone else. As the years go by, human lives become cluttered and crowded with the debris of the past: old loves, old hatreds, confining habits, obligations that are no longer justified, unrewarding relationships that survive because of compromise, routine or fear. We have to learn to let go of what is already gone or of what is no longer needed. If you are going to do magic to obtain something that you need or want, you are going to have to clear a space or make room for it in your life. This is difficult. Much of what we retain but can no longer use is retained by strong positive or negative feelings.

In the magical tradition, personal sacrifice has always played an important role. This sacrifice has nothing in common with hatred of the body or with a rejection of pleasure and eroticism. For example, coven members fast and/or give up something before a ceremony. This sacrifice involves giving up of what you have, or letting go of who you are, in order to clear a space within your being. If you do not clear a space, then you are in the situation of someone who is green and does magic to become blue — the result is that you become turquoise. If you dissolve who you are, and become a space, then when you do magic to become blue, you fill the space and become blue.

For example, let us say that you desire to own a Lexus. But behind your desire, you believe that you will only get a Volkswagen, or that your magical action will fail. You believe this, because you feel that is all that you deserve, or because all your friends have V.W.s or because your parents have always told you to be practical and drive a car that has good gas mileage. If this is your situation, then your attempt to do magic to get a Lexus will be impaired by your previous programming. Consciously you are working to get a Lexus, but unconsciously you are working to get a V.W., and the unconscious always wins. So it is essential to dissolve all previous programming (ideas, feelings, attitudes) and clear a space. You do this by dissolving both the desire and its opposite. As Denning and Phillips say, "it is good ... to practice destroying unwanted images" (Denning and Phillips, 1980: 119).

Clearing a Space I

1. Experience wanting the Lexus, feel it, hear it, experience it completely. See yourself driving that Lexus.

2. Expand, intensify, or increase this experience until it will go no further.

3. Step out of this experience. See it, give it a form, a shape. Experience the separation between yourself and this bundle of ideas and feelings.

4. Realize that this experience is not you.

5. Now allow it to clear, explode, or burn. Let it go, release it.

6. Repeat steps 1 through 5, until you can no longer experience the reality in step 2.

Clearing a Space II

1. Experience resisting the Lexus, not getting the Lexus. Experience all the thoughts and feelings that you do not deserve to get a Lexus and that you should not get a Lexus. Experience all the thoughts and feelings that your magical action will fail to get a Lexus.

2. Expand, intensify, increase this experience until it will go no further.

3. Step out of this experience. See it, give it a shape, a form. Experience the separation between yourself and this bundle of negative thoughts and feelings.

4. Realize that this experience is not you.

5. Now allow it to clear, explode, or burn. Let it go, release it.

You have cleared a space by releasing the desire or longing to have a Lexus and all thoughts for or against it. You have released the feelings of not deserving a Lexus, and all resistance to having it. You have cleared or released the polar opposites of a desire and the resistance or opposition to that desire. There is now a space in your being. That space can be filled by your magical will and the results of your magical action. We suggest that before doing magic, you prepare by clearing a space in your being, once a day, for several days. You will know when this preparation is completed because you will reach a point where you feel "no change." At this point, you are ready.

YOUR MAGICAL POTENTIAL:
THE SPHERE OF AVAILABILITY

On the next issue, we explain the same thing in different ways.

Angelique's View:

We come into this life to learn certain lessons and go through certain experiences. It is as if, before birth, we choose a stage which is set with props and actors and then we choose the role which we are going to play. We can select among many possible roles, but certain experiences are only accessible from a given role. Other people and the material furniture of the world are objectively real, but we have chosen the mode of interaction and the role we play. The choice you made to be born into a specific lifetime as a certain person of a given gender, in a given country, in a given economic class, with a specific set of potential talents and a specific lack of potential abilities establishes the objective givens that you have. Magic is not a wish-fulfilling gem in a fairy tale. Beyond your objective givens, what you can obtain through magic depends on how much energy you can attract and manipulate. In practice, this process seems to be incremental.

George's View:

What Angelique describes as an incremental process of attracting energy, is what I call your sphere of availability (Ophiel, 1972: 25-34). Your sphere of availability is determined by:

   a. What you have right now;

   b. Your current capacity to make room or clear a space within your being.

The point here is that you aim for the next increment. *You do not overreach.* As your magic works, and the desired item arrives in your life, this *enlarges* your sphere of availability.

To do magic successfully, you focus on a *visualization of the final outcome.* The specific details of just *how* the final outcome will come about, is up to the natural flow and wisdom of the inner forces. Your sole task is to concentrate on the final outcome. Clairvoyants explain that this exclusive focus on a desired final outcome is necessary because of mirror-inversions in the inner planes. Directions are inverted, and sequences flow from effect to cause, rather than the other way around. As Franz Bardon says, the language of the inner planes is made up of *images*, not words or numbers (Bardon, 1975: 79, 102).

In visualizing the final outcome, specify how you will feel, what you will be experiencing and what it looks like. For example, consider love magic. Rather than doing magic to obtain a specific person, specify that you want someone with whom you will be very much in love, who will love you and with whom you will be very happy. If you do love magic to obtain a specific person, you run the risk that that person will be unsuitable or will make you unhappy. Another example: it would be unwise to do magic to obtain a million dollars because you might get the million dollars and the IRS might take away most of it. Instead, do magic to pay off all your debts or to become comfortably wealthy.

Finally, we have the related problem of retaining what we get. The final outcome, thing, or condition comes to you from the inner planes in a kind of flowing tide. If you ignore it, the same tide will take it away. To keep what you receive through your magical efforts, you need to *bind* it. You bind something by starting to *use it* as soon as possible.

To do magic effectively you need to contact a source of shamanic or magical power. To tap such a source, you need to enter an altered state of consciousness. Here we find three possibilities:

a. You can tap the power of your power animal.

b. You can use the power generated by sexual arousal and release.

c. You can use ritual or ceremonial magic, and learn to invoke the Watchtowers and the cone of power.

To do magic with your power animal, you go on a shamanic inner journey with the aid of the appropriate monotonous sonic input. You face your power animal and make a single request, both in words and as a visualized final outcome. After the journey, you empty your mind and think about something else. This cut-off is very important. You have just sent a psychic projectile into the inner planes to bring you something or change something in your life. If you think about it or talk about it, you are only draining its energy. As the Jungians say, daydreaming is debilitating and works against integration.

SEX MAGIC

Sex magic is also very effective and available to almost everyone. Furthermore, you can do it alone (namely, without the knowledge of your partner), or you can do it jointly. During sexual activity we enter an altered state of consciousness. Both partners exchange energy, and at the moment of climax there is a merging of both auras or energy fields (Mumford, 1988: 40). During repeated sexual encounters, both partners share more and more of their energy fields which is a good reason for being very selective.

The technology of sex magic is as follows: You visualize a final outcome, thing or condition which you need or want. You hold this visualization through arousal and then release it at the moment of orgasm. Then you empty your mind, let it go, and you think about something completely different.

In summary, the practice of magic requires that you:

1. Relax and enter an altered state of consciousness;

2. Tap a source of (shamanic or magical) energy or power;

3. Visualize the final outcome;

4. Focus your magical will (or unity of desire) on that visualization;

5. Release it, or let it go.

Unconsciously, this sequence is followed by those who engage in successful prayer. No gods have answered their request, but they have made the right moves. They have entered an altered state of consciousness. They have tapped the energy of one of the artificial elementals (e.g., the Virgin Mary or the Goddess Tara) associated with a particular religion. They have visualized the final outcome. Finally, they have focused the unified desire of their entire being on that outcome.

A HISTORY OF WESTERN MAGICAL TRADITION

It is a major argument of this book that the entire esoteric tradition of both East and West originated with the shamanism of the hunters and gatherers. Since both Wicca and Ceremonial Magic have shamanic origins, their practitioners can enhance the power and effectiveness of their inner journeys and rituals by borrowing neo-shamanic techniques. Likewise, as inheritors of magical traditions that span more than 6,000 years, contemporary neo-shamans can increase the effectiveness of their practice by incorporating historical developments such as the theory of the elements, the elemental weapons, invoking and banishing pentagrams, words of power and the use of the Kabbalah to awaken the energy centers.

Magic reached contemporary Western civilization in two forms: the ritual or ceremonial magicians and the Witches. From the Renaissance on, ritual magicians such as Ficino, Pico della Mirandola, Agrippa, or Dee, were scholarly, university educated, solitary male practitioners who made an effort to place their activities in a Judeo-Christian framework. As such, they were ignored or condemned, but rarely persecuted or exterminated. Giordano Bruno was burned at the stake because he had the temerity to openly advocate pagan Hermeticism over Christianity (Yates, 1969: 230).

The appearance of the Golden Dawn in late 19th century Victorian England, signaled a change. For the first time we get an *organization* of ritual magicians. From 1888 – 1896 the Golden Dawn initiated 315 members, of which 119, or approximately one third, were women (Howe, 1972: 49). Furthermore, while the Golden Dawn retained a solid core of Masonic and Rosicrucian (Protestant) Christianity, MacGregor Mathers added Celtic, Greco-Roman and Egyptian deities. The process of separation from Christian symbols and beliefs has continued. Today, an order of British magicians holds that magical abilities "can be developed without any symbolic system except reality itself" (Carroll, 1987: 7).

Contemporary Witchcraft or Wicca shares some features with medieval Witchcraft. It is pagan, it is organized in small groups, and it is largely female. Its pagan character alone explains persecution and extermination, quite aside from the Satanist fantasies of Inquisitors and others. The romantic and fanciful claims that the Craft is an organized survivor from a remote, pre-Christian past (i.e., Margaret Murray, Gerald Gardner) are only matched by the tedious disclaimers of professional skeptics (Adler, 1986: 45-66). As of this moment, the romantics seem to be ahead. British historian Michael Harrison discovered that the "nonsense" chants of British covens are in *Basque* - a non-Indo-European language - and refer to a period of the Neolithic era in which animals were starting to be domesticated (Harrison, 1974: 152-175). Furthermore, contemporary Renaissance historian Carlo Ginzburg has argued that the ecstasy or altered state of consciousness, the magical journey, and the human-into-animal transformations found in early 15th century accounts of the Witches' sabbath, are all of shamanic origin (Ginzburg, 1991: 257, 300).

The modern Wiccan movement, with numerous covens in the United States, Britain, France, Holland, and Germany, is "an atavistic resurgence of staggering proportions" (Mumford, 1988: 105) in that it represents a return to its source: Gnosticism and shamanism. In line with the expected anarchistic ethos, there is no orthodoxy. Nevertheless, covens in England and America share the worship of a mother Goddess, identified with the Earth or the Moon, and the worship of a horned God who is lord of the animals. The mother is love and nurturing. The father is the lord of karma and death. Here we have the Freudian eros and thanatos, as well as the Gnostic concern with gender parity. As lord of the animals, the God is the first shaman. The Craft is a fertility religion, much concerned with ecology, the seasons, and the phases of the moon.

Some covens observe ritual nudity. The famous Dutch historian J. Huizinga describes a small painting by an unknown master associated with the followers of Jan van Eyck. In the picture a nude girl engages in magical practices to summon her lover (Huizinga, 1954: 315). This 15th century Dutch painting is evidence that, contrary to the claims of his critics, Gerald Gardner did not invent the association between ritual nudity and Witchcraft. Some covens incorporate sexual intercourse by priest and priestess as part of the ceremony. Others retain this sexual symbolism only at a ritual level: The priest says: "As the athame [dagger] is to the male..." and the priestess responds: "So is the cup to the female." The athame is then inserted into the wine cup. The word "athame" comes from the Greek *athanatos*, the immortal or undying (Harrison, 1974: 156), and involves an obvious celebration of virility.

THE ELEMENTAL WEAPONS

To do ritual or ceremonial magic you will need to obtain, purchase, or manufacture the four ceremonial tools or weapons which represent the elements: the pentacle, the cup, the dagger, and the wand. Think of these weapons as tools of consciousness for energy exchanges with the inner planes. Aside from correct measurements, the main consideration should be aesthetic. Ritual magic is an art, and its weapons should be beautiful to see and pleasurable to hold.

The pentacle represents the element Earth, and makes up your ceremonial altar. It is a wooden board, three-fourths of an inch thick, approximately 12 by 12 inches square, and made of Oak. On one surface you will draw, incise, or burn a double circle with an enclosed pentagram or five-pointed star, tip up. The diameter of the outer circle is nine and five-eighths inches. The diameter of the inner circle is six and five-eighths inches. The inner circle is divided into five equal segments and the pentagram is inscribed inside of it. Make sure that the fifth or upper arm of the pentagram is aligned with the center of the board. When in operation, this fifth arm will point North. Your pentacle should look like figure twenty-one.

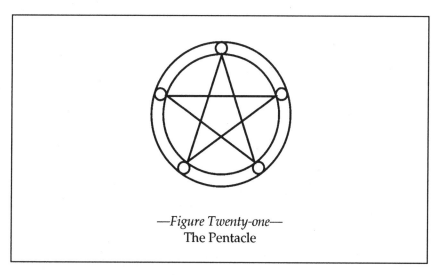

—*Figure Twenty-one*—
The Pentacle

The double circle contains five, equidistant small circles, aligned with the tips of the pentagram. These are the positions for small candleholders which will hold five candles. These candles should be approximately seven to nine inches long. The candles must be of the same color. We suggest that you start with a set that is all-white. When the ceremony starts, the flames of these five candles will represent the fifth element or Ether. These five flames enclose a spatial pentagram within which the Void may manifest as either brilliant light or awesome darkness. Your pentacle is used for synthesis, assembly, and earthing. It is here that you will visualize your desired final outcome, thing, or condition.

The ceremonial cup represents the element Water. It should be made of wood or silver or silver-plated and about seven and a half inches tall. The cup is associated with the mother Goddess, and it will contain wine. The cup is used for receiving and containing *feelings*.

The ceremonial steel dagger represents the element Fire (King and Skinner, 1976: 60–61). It should be approximately nine inches long (the handle, three inches; the blade, six inches). The dagger or athame is used for banishing, destruction, and undoing.

The ceremonial wand represents the element Air. It should be approximately 12 to 20 inches long (Bardon, 1975: 36). The original wand is made of wood. We get excellent results with a wand of rock crystal or quartz. The wand is for invoking, evoking, and for concentrating the magical will.

In addition, you will need wine for the cup and some bread or cake on a small dish. You will also need to burn some incense. We suggest sandalwood, Himalayan musk, cedar, or sage. The purpose of incense is to help clear the area of any entities that are not summoned.

SYMBOLISM

The symbolism is from Shamanic Wicca, that is to say, a Craft ceremony that has been refashioned to invoke its powerful shamanic origins. We use a polar arrangement of the elements. Three of the Watchtowers are shamanic power animals. The fourth Watchtower is personified as a human female who represents the Moon. She is a pregnant mother, who is scantily dressed in scarf-like, clinging and flowing clothes. We observe gender parity: two of the Watchtowers are male and two are female.

EAST: The element is Fire, symbolized by invoking a pentagram of *red* flame. Inside the pentagram blazes the morning Sun. It is Spring. The Watchtower is a gigantic orange-red male *Lion*. This is the domain of aggression, bravery, and courage.

SOUTH: The element is Earth, symbolized by invoking a pentagram of *white* flame. There is a sensation of summer heat. Inside the pentagram is a scene of white sand. The Watchtower is a gigantic, white, female *Bear*. She sits on her hind legs and has a sense of humor. This is the domain of life and material things.

WEST: The element is Water, symbolized by invoking a pentagram of *green* flame. It is fall or autumn. Inside the pentagram is a scene of a blue-green ocean which changes into the ocean at night with a full Moon. The Watchtower is a human female, the pregnant *Mother*. This is the domain of love and nurturing.

NORTH: The element is Air, symbolized by an invoking pentagram of *black* flame. It is winter and there is a sensation of cold wind. Inside the pentagram is a scene of a storm over the Himalayas. The Watchtower is a gigantic, male, purple *Eagle*. This is the domain of death and release into the inner planes.

PRACTICE SIX

Assuming that you have been diligently practicing the Middle Pillar exercise for several months, you are now ready to learn how to perform a ceremony of ritual magic. The energy generated by this ceremony can be used to learn, to balance and to heal, and to do magic. Begin by locking the doors, drawing the shades or curtains, unplugging the phone and insuring total safety and privacy. This means that a house is ideal, while an apartment with neighbors is second best. Your ceremony is going to be done at night, on or just before the full Moon. Night and darkness favor shamanism and magical operations. At night, the Yin energy makes it easier to go inward. During the day, the outward flowing Yang energy makes this difficult. The full Moon indicates that the power of the Earth is at a maximum.

1. The position of the magician is in the South, facing North, with your altar in front of you. Your cup with wine, a dish with bread, and your athame (dagger) and wand should be assembled between you and the altar. Light the incense on a dish on the side of the altar. Light the candles as if drawing an *invoking* pentagram of flame as shown in figure twenty-two.

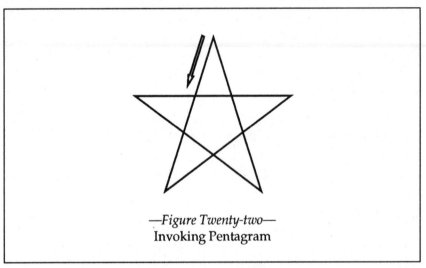

—*Figure Twenty-two*—
Invoking Pentagram

Spend a few minutes of no-thought staring quietly at the center of the pentagram of flame. If others are with you, then hold hands and circulate energy clockwise. The energy comes in through the right hand, which is held palm up-ward, and leaves through the left hand which is held palm downward.

2. Take the athame (dagger) and walk clockwise around your altar to the East. Face East and hold the athame with both hands. Starting above your head, with the first stroke

toward your right foot, draw a banishing pentagram of white light as shown in figure twenty-three.

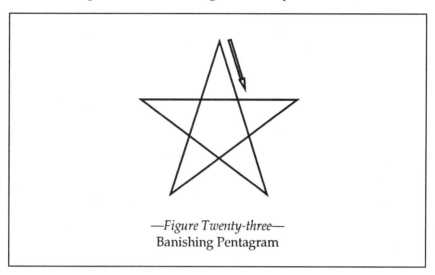

—*Figure Twenty-three*—
Banishing Pentagram

As you do this, vibrate-chant YOD - HEH - VAU - HEH. Stab the center and visualize the pentagram moving away from you, cleaning the area. Repeat this three times.

3. Go to the South and draw three banishing pentagrams of white light. Go to the West and draw three banishing pentagrams of white light. Go to the North and draw three banishing pentagrams of white light. Return clockwise to your post in the South.

4. Standing in the South, facing North, hold your wand above your head with your right arm. Your left arm should be extended, pointing to the center of the altar. Activate number one (sefira Keter), in blazing white light, above your head. Vibrate-chant EH - HEH - YEH a few times.

5. Now, you are going to invoke the Watchtowers, starting in the East. Hold the wand in your right hand, above your head. Your left arm will be down and back, pointing to the altar behind you. At each cardinal point you will draw an invoking pentagram in blazing color. You will

start at the top of your head, and your first stroke will be toward your left foot as shown in figure twenty-four. You will vibrate - chant EH - HEH - YEH and stab the center.

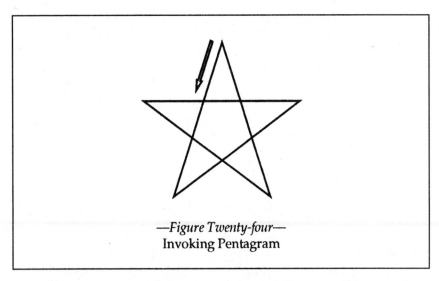

—*Figure Twenty-four*—
Invoking Pentagram

6. The pentagram of the East is in red flame. A blazing Sun is inside of it. Behind and above it comes the gigantic orange-red Lion. Wand above your head, chant:

> *Holy Watchtower of the East, great Lion, fire, Sun, we do call and summon thee forth to come and witness our rite, lend us thy aid, and guard us against all intrusions that might come from the East.*

Vibrate - chant the word of power: EH - VOR, HEH - VOR - HEH. "Blessed be." Finish with "So mote it be."

7. The pentagram of the South is in blazing white flame. Hot, white sand is inside it. Behind and above comes the gigantic, white, mother Bear. Wand above your head, chant:

> *Holy Watchtower of the South, great mother Bear, Earth, life, we do call and summon thee forth to witness our rite, lend us thy aid, and guard us against all intrusions that might come from the South.*

Vibrate - chant the word of power. Finish with: "Blessed be. So mote it be."

8. The pentagram of the West is in green flame. In the center is a blue-green ocean, followed by the ocean at night with the full Moon above. Behind and above it comes the pregnant Mother. Wand above your head, chant:

> *Holy Watchtower of the West, blue-green water, ocean, Moon, holy Mother, we do call and summons thee forth to witness our rite, lend us thy aid and guard us against all intrusions that might come from the West.*

Vibrate-chant the word of power. Finish with "Blessed be. So mote it be."

9. The pentagram of the North is in blazing black flame. In the center, cold wind, darkness, snow and ice. Behind and above it comes the gigantic purple eagle. Wand above your head, chant:

> *Holy Watchtower of the North, great purple Eagle, cold air, wind, darkness, death, we do call and summons thee forth to witness our rite, lend us thy aid, and guard us against all intrusions that might come from the North.*

Vibrate-chant the word of power. Finish with "Blessed be. So mote it be."

Return to the East and say "The circle is closed." Move clockwise to your position in the South, facing North.

If a clairvoyant is present, he or she can usually see the arrival of the Watchtowers. If you are working with a group, it is good to bring each Watchtower into a person so members of the group can feel and experience that energy. When doing the ceremony alone, you go to each quarter to feel and experience the energy of the Watchtower. For example, in the South you feel strength. The West teaches you how to deal with your emotions and how to feel emotions; so if you are having a hard time, or feel no emotions, sitting and meditating in the West is very good. The North teaches you about letting go, about dying and about psychic things. It is a great experience to sit in the North. In the East you learn about bravery and courage; you learn how to deal with your anger and aggression.

10. Do the Middle Pillar exercise to bring down the cone of power. After the Circulation of the Body of Light, visualize the cone in astral blue, spinning clockwise, as it descends and encloses the magic circle.

11. Extend your arms upward, at a 45 degree angle, and invoke the Goddess and the God. You are using the cone of power to establish communication and asking to share in their energy. We ask the Mother for love and nurturing. We ask the Father for wisdom, and that we may learn our (karmic) lessons quickly. The Mother is Yin energy, like psychic energy. The Father is Yang energy, or action.

We have said that you "invoke" the God and the Goddess, but we mean something quite different. The energy of the Goddess and the God will not come down to you. You have to go up to them. You do this by raising your energy level to make contact with their energy level. This is not easy, and at first it will probably seem impossible. Therefore, instructions on how to do this will be given at the end of chapter seven. Even without actual contact with the energy level of the God and Goddess this ceremony is an extraordinarily effective ritual vehicle for the practice of magic.

12. Consecrate the bread by raising it up with both hands:

> *Holy Father, bless this bread. We feed others, that we, too, may be fed.*

The bread stands for knowledge and wisdom. If you give of what you have, then you open a space within yourself to receive more. If you teach what you know, then you open a space to receive more knowledge. Consecrate the wine by raising the wine cup with both hands:

Holy Mother, bless this wine.

The wine represents love.

13. Standing, arms extended downward and pointing to the pentacle of flame on the altar, visualize the final outcome, thing, or condition which you need or want. If others are with you, they too stand and point to the center. Then, palms down, slowly raise your arms. As you do so, visualize that the final outcome enters a zone of red color, then a zone of orange color, then a zone of yellow color, then a zone of green color, then a zone of blue color. As the scene of the final outcome enters a zone of purple color, you shout and release the cone. Shouting, laughing, screaming, or crying are physical ways of letting go. Therefore, shouting or screaming are essential for the complete release of the cone of power.

    Then you ground the energy that is left within the circle by placing both hands on the floor or ground. Then you sit quietly for a moment, and regenerate and recover your energy balance. It is like having an orgasm. After an orgasm, you stop, you rest, you relax, you experience the energy of love and gentleness. You have to regroup and experience again. You do this by holding hands and circulating the energy in a clockwise direction. While doing this, you want to become completely still, and yet allow the energy to continue to flow through you. By doing this, you experience what it is like to be in a moment between moments or in the space between thoughts.

14. If the ceremony is being conducted by a priestess and a priest, then the priest raises the athame tip down and says "As the athame is to the male." The priestess holds the wine cup and says "So is the cup to the female." The priest inserts the dagger into the wine.

15. Share the bread and the wine going clockwise. Starting with the person to the left of the priestess, each person, by turn, asks the person to the left "Will you share a bite of bread with me in honor of the Father?" The recipient responds "Yes, I will." The first person places a small bit of bread between the recipient's lips. The recipient says "To the Father. Blessed be."

    A slightly different pattern is used to share the wine. The Priestess asks the person on her left,"Will you share a sip of wine with me in honor of the Mother?" The person answers, "Yes, I will." The Priestess then takes the first sip of wine, and hands the cup to the first person, and says "To the Mother. Blessed be." The love of the Mother begins in the Priestess, and then goes outward. The Priestess takes the first sip of wine to symbolize that one must first love oneself to be able to love others.

16. Now you are going to thank and dismiss the Watchtowers. Take your athame and walk clockwise to the East.

    > *Holy Watchtower of the East, red fire, Sun, holy Lion. We thank thee, and as thou dost return to thy lovely realm, we bid thee, Hail and farewell! Hail and farewell! Hail and farewell!*

    You use your athame to draw a banishing pentagram. The group chants "Hail and farewell!"

    Go to the South and repeat the same thing:

    > *Holy Watchtower of the South, earth, life, holy mother Bear. We thank thee, and as thou dost return to thy lovely realm, we bid thee, Hail and farewell! Hail and farewell! Hail and farewell!*

    As you say "Hail and farewell", draw your banishing pentagram.

Go to the West and do the same thing. Go to the North and do the same thing. Return to the East and say "The circle is open." Snuff out the flames of the candles, but do *not* blow them out. In this context, blowing out candles disturbs the energy field, creating an imbalance, diffusion, or a scattering. You can allow the candles to burn down completely. You can give the candles to other members of the group and ask that they take them home and burn then down completely. Wax absorbs magical energy, and it is necessary to burn the candles down completely to release that energy. If you use dripless candles, that is the end. If you use ordinary candles then the remaining wax should be buried in the earth.

17. People come to this ceremony after having bathed and fasted. Fasting is another way of making a space within yourself in order to receive more of what you need. Once the ceremony is finished, food and wine follows. This rejoicing is a way of saying "Thank you."

CHAPTER SEVEN

THE
MANTIC METHODS

The occult tradition suggests that we should assume personal responsibility for our present incarnation. There are no accidents. Where others see blind chance and probability, the occultist sees a lesson to be learned. We are perfectly aware that we live in a world of political oppression, economic exploitation, and raw evil. A fight against any of these is part of learning one's lesson. But more often than not, most of the vicissitudes that affect a human life are not the big issues, but relatively smaller concerns: personal betrayal, an unsatisfactory job, a health problem, loss of love. The magical viewpoint suggests that you consider everything that happens to you as a personal message from the universe, or as a comment on how you are living your life (Carroll, 1987: 49).

As Gnostics, namely those who rely on knowledge and not on faith, we need foreknowledge of what is coming into our lives from the inner planes. Such foreknowledge taps the outcome, thing, or condition, while it is in process of becoming and not yet fully determinate. It becomes fully determinate, only when it reaches the material plane and happens. The whole point of foreknowledge is to tap the outcome before it becomes final and while we still have a chance to change it or stop it by a change of behavior or by the use of magic.

The *mantic* or divinatory methods are procedures for trying to obtain foreknowledge. Of course, if you are a high grade clairvoyant, or fortunate enough to have such a friend, then you do not need to use any mantic procedures. Unfortunately, such gifted individuals are rare and in constant danger of being worked to death by the needs and demands of their friends.

Mantic methods are of two sorts: open-ended and close-ended. Open-ended methods, such as Tarot, *I Ching*, or Geomancy, are like algebraic equations with two unknowns (an X and a Y). To work them successfully you need intuition or a touch of clairvoyance. They are like the proverbial computer whose negative instance is described as garbage in and garbage out. In other words, you are dealing with a procedure where the quality of output will be determined by the quality of input.

Close-ended mantic methods such as Astrology or Palmistry start with a known, clearly specifiable, material state of affairs: a configuration of planets at birth or the lines on the palm of the hand. However, the outcome still requires interpretation, and this requires intuition. The role of intuition and clairvoyance in a close-ended method such as Palmistry, can be seen when we examine the distance that separates the legendary exploits of the famous Cheiro (Louis Hamon) and the rules and instructions contained in his excellent books. If you study his books (Cheiro, 1929; Cheiro, 1931), you will learn Palmistry. With considerable practice, you will become quite good at it. However, unless you are a clairvoyant, it is unrealistic to expect that you can match Cheiro's extraordinary performance. Cheiro's written work is completely reliable with only one exception: the fingers of the hand are associated with elements, not with planets. The thumb is Water, the index finger is Fire, the middle finger is Aether or the fifth element, the ring finger is Earth and the little finger is Air (Bardon, 1981: 102).

ON ASTROLOGY

Sidereal Astrology corrects for precession of the equinoxes. It uses a zodiac of 12, 30-degree divisions of the ecliptic, anchored in the constellations. As developed in England by Roy Firebrace and Cyril Fagan (Fagan and Firebrace, 1971) and in the United States by Donald Bradley (Bradley, 1973), it is an excellent divinatory device. This is so, particularly after we add the contributions of France's Michel Gauquelin: the statistical discovery of the true foreground or strong areas of the chart (Gauquelin, 1988: 251-253), the statistical demonstration that the Tropical zodiac is worthless, the statistical demonstration that houses are meaningless in a natal chart, and the statistical demonstration that natal charts do not show insanity or psychopathology.

For predictive charts, such as Solar Returns, we recommend the use of equal house from the Ascendant, for three reasons:

1. The houses are a purely mantic device with no astronomical counterpart;

2. All areas of life should be equally represented; and

3. We need to prevent Pluto from wandering into the wrong house through declination.

To avoid self-delusion and so-called predictions after the fact it is important to limit our consideration to the three most powerful aspects — conjunction, opposition, square — with tight orbs of no more than seven degrees. Furthermore, the raw data for birth charts should be unrectified information from public archives such as those found in cities, municipalities, or hospitals.

A Sidereal birth chart makes no predictions. If properly drawn and based on accurate data it gives a psychological portrait of the person. This portrait is for approximately age 20 — the end of adolescence. It represents the combined effects of nature and nurture, genetic endowment and socialization in family and environment.

In terms of the Cartesian-Newtonian assumptions of scientific positivism, this claim is an absurd scandal. Yet the truth of this claim can be verified by anyone who takes the trouble to do so. How this is possible, we do not know. The relative, geocentric position of the Sun, Moon, and planets at birth is a verifiable astronomical fact. Science has found no energy from the planets that could possibly account for astrological effects. Furthermore, the Sun, Moon, and planets are also the Greco-Roman gods, the Gnostic archons, the sefirot and the archetypes of Jung's collective unconscious. We do not know if we are dealing with purely external, astronomical entities, or with internal entities of the unconscious psyche, or with both.

Sidereal astrology focuses on solar returns as predictive charts. The predictions are verifiable, but not completely determinate, which is precisely what we want. Every year, around your birthday, the sun returns to the exact position it had at your birth. A sidereal chart done for this moment predicts some events and conditions that will affect your life during the following year. But this is only half the information. The other half is obtained by doing a converse solar return, which is a chart done for a moment of the remote past before your birth. For example, if this is your 40th birthday, a chart done for your birth sun position 40 years *before your birth*, contains information about events and conditions that will affect your life during the current year. The implications of this absurdity are staggering. We seem to be dealing with time sequences which flow both forward and *backward* from the moment of birth.

It is of some historical interest that between 1908 and 1912, a founder of the Golden Dawn, S. L. MacGregor Mathers, developed a system of sidereal astrology. He rejected the tropical zodiac with its fictional signs and changed to a zodiac of the constellations (King, 1970: 203). But 1908 was eight years too late, since the order disintegrated after 1900 following a revolt of the membership and the expulsion of Mathers. Had Mathers turned to sidereal astrology while he was still the head of the Golden Dawn, and had the sidereal zodiac replaced the tropical zodiac in the teaching of the Order, the mainstream of Western astrology would probably be quite different.

If you want to explore sidereal astrology, we suggest that you delegate computations to a reliable computer service, such as the one organized by the late Neil F. Michelsen:

Astro Computing Services Inc.
P.O. Box 34487
San Diego, California, 92163 – 4487

1. To obtain a natal chart, send them your exact birth data: place, time, day, month, year. Request a natal chart that uses:

    a. Equal House from the Ascendant

    b. Sidereal zodiac (Fagan's Ayanamsa)

    Send them four dollars (as of Spring, 1991).

2. To interpret a natal chart you will need to obtain a book that is fairly hard to get:

    Cyril Fagan and R. C. Firebrace. 1971. *Primer of Sidereal Astrology*. Isabella, Missouri: Littlejohn Publishing Co.

3. The computer printout from Astro Computing Services will contain too much information, some of it of dubious value. Ignoring items such as midpoints, part of fortune, nodes, etc., we suggest that you concentrate on the essential information: sidereal planetary positions, planetary aspects — conjunction, opposition, square, only — with orbs up to seven degrees. You may want to transcribe this information on to a new chart wheel divided into 12 equal parts. Then use the Fagan-Firebrace to interpret the aspects.

4. In a Sidereal Natal chart, the mantic device of Houses is of no relevance, but Sidereal Zodiac Sun signs must be considered. The meaning of Sidereal Sun signs is as follows:

NATAL SUN IN:

ARIES: Ambitious, fond of power and authority.

LIBRA: Not interested in power, artistic, a peacemaker.

TAURUS: Tolerant, gentle, mild, patient, hates violence.

SCORPIO: Outspoken, daring, rash. Loves to fight.

GEMINI: Changeable views and beliefs, restless, versatile.

SAGITTARIUS: Fixed views and beliefs. Judgmental.

CANCER: Imaginative, fantasizes that his/her life is different. Generous with money.

CAPRICORN: Realistic, feels that his/her lot will remain the same. Tight with money.

LEO: Proud elitist, very selective of people.

AQUARIUS: Egalitarian, rejects all differences of race, class, nationality.

VIRGO: Seeks back stage. Self-effacing. Fond of diets.

PISCES: Loves center stage, theatrical. Loves good food and wine.

Notice that the meanings are organized as dualities or polar oppositions. Unlike Tropical Sun signs, Sidereal Sun signs provide only one or two units of information. Add this to the information you get from aspects to make up a personality portrait. In describing this portrait, avoid vague generalities (e.g, you are sensitive), avoid statements that are true by definition and refuse to embroider or generalize. Finally, it is a good idea to do some hard reality testing: ask your client to confirm or discomfirm each one of your statements.

The statistical studies of Michel Gauquelin (Gauquelin, 1988: 20-21) have demonstrated that the strong areas of a horoscope chart are *not* houses one, four, seven, and ten (as tradition would have it). The investigations of Gauquelin show that for a 12-fold, equal house division from the Ascendant, the strong areas are as follows:

Alpha Areas:

1. All of house 12 and 10 degrees of house one.

2. Thirty degrees to the right of the M.C., and ten degrees to the left.

Beta Areas:

1. Last 20 degrees of house six, and five degrees of house seven.

2. Fifteen degrees to the left of the I.C., and five degrees to the right.

This follows tradition only to the extent that the Alpha areas show that the strongest zone is around the Ascendant and the M.C. The relatively weaker Beta areas pinpoint the Descendant and the I.C. Although the meaning of houses seems to be irrelevant for natal charts, aspects made by bodies located in the Alpha or Beta areas will be particularly salient.

If you want to explore predictive charts or sidereal solar returns, you will have to obtain two charts: one that goes forward in time and one that goes back in time. Solar return charts are computed for your current place of residence (not your birthplace). Before you contact Astro Computing Services, you will have to figure out which is the relevant year back in time. For example, let us pretend that you became age 20 on May 15, 1990. This means that you were born on May 15, 1970. It also means that your solar return back in time will be for 1950 (20 years before your birth).

1. Ask Astro Computing Services for two solar return charts
    a. Equal House
    b. Sidereal zodiac (Fagan's Ayanamsa)
    c. For your current city or town of residence.

2. Tell them that the first solar return is for 1990, and that the second one is for 1950.

3. These two charts are to be computed for your sidereal Sun position (the same one that appears in your sidereal natal chart). Send them eight dollars (as of Spring, 1991).

4. To interpret your solar returns, you will need to obtain the following paperback:
    Donald A. Bradley. 1973. *Solar and Lunar Returns*. St. Paul, MN: Llewellyn Publications.

5. Transcribe the relevant information from the Astro Computing printouts, and interpret following Bradley. Remember, unlike the case for natal charts, zodiac signs are largely irrelevant, but the mantic device of Houses is fully applicable to solar returns. The meaning of Houses is as follows in the chart on the next page:

    Once again, notice that the basic meanings of the Houses are organized as polar opposites. The houses represent areas of life, and they are a kind of background to the aspects (as in the figure and ground relationship of Gestalt psychology). For example, let us say that one of your Solar Return charts contains a rather sinister Saturn-Neptune conjunction. This aspect means "worry, fatigue, and some kind of removal (exile, deportation)." If it appears in house four, the home, it means that you will experience some kind of removal in or from your home (e.g., having to vacate for a few days while insects are exterminated). However, if this same aspect appears in house ten, occupation/profession, then you are in real danger of being terminated or fired from your job. The specific way in which the aspect is likely to manifest, cannot be judged in advance.

HOUSE MEANINGS

HOUSE ONE:
  The self.

HOUSE TWO:
  Money.

HOUSE THREE:
  Communications. Short
  journeys. Relatives.

HOUSE FOUR:
  The home (The Mother).

HOUSE FIVE:
  Love-given, sex, creativity,
  art, pleasures, children.

HOUSE SIX:
  Work, health.

HOUSE SEVEN:
  Other people (public, clients,
  audience). Partnerships.

HOUSE EIGHT:
  Property. Secrecy, Esoteric
  concerns.

HOUSE NINE:
  High culture. Long journeys.

HOUSE TEN: Occupation/Pro-
  fession. (The Father).

HOUSE ELEVEN:
  Love-received. Friends.

HOUSE TWELVE:
  Institutions.

The mantic methods, including astrological predictive charts such as Solar Returns, do not predict the occurrence of specific life events, but rather, *categories of events*. For example, a Moon-Saturn conjunction foretells some kind of loss, deprivation, setback, grief, or bereavement, including such events as loss of a friend, being victimized by theft, or the death of a relative or loved one. Even in the case of death, the aspect does not distinguish between the *pro forma* bereavement over a distant cousin, and the truly devastating bereavement over a much loved significant other. The explanation for this lack of specificity is that the mantic procedure detects the event as it comes to our lives from the inner planes and while it is still partly indeterminate. The event becomes fully determinate only as it happens in the ordinary material world. In a sense, this indeterminacy can be an asset. It means that there is still time for us to do something to alter the course of future events. There is still time to interfere and head off the threatening eventuality, or reduce its malignancy.

A coming nemesis usually signals that there is some lesson that we have to learn. So, the first thing to do is to find out the nature of the lesson. For this purpose, do a journey, and ask your power animal. Once you learn the lesson, then act to head off the potentially painful coming event.

ON THE I CHING AND THE CHINESE ELEMENTS

When we turn to the open-ended mantic methods, such as the *I Ching* or the Tarot, we observe that a minimal requirement is that the reader enter an altered state of consciousness. This is the whole point behind preliminary maneuvers such as counting yarrow sticks, throwing coins, or shuffling and dividing the deck of cards into three stacks and then feeling their energy with the palm of the hand. In a lesser known method such as Geomancy, the reader enters an altered state of consciousness by the preliminary evocation of the Earth elementals. The purpose of the altered state of consciousness is to bring forth the reader's special talents or intuition. Without this altered state of consciousness, the reading remains a purely mechanical operation with trivial or chance results.

The *I Ching* originated around 1000 B.C.E., at the time when the Chou dynasty replaced the Shang. The 64 hexagrams seem to describe a nobleman's rise to power (Whincup, 1986: 2), and they are full of references to legendary and historical events of the time (Huang, 1985: 11–20, 37, 43–52). In our opinion, the best translation for mantic purposes is that of M. I. T. physicist Kerson Huang and his poet wife Rosemary Huang (Huang, Kerson and Rosemary Huang.

1985. *I Ching*. New York: Workman Publishing). The Huang translation has two decisive advantages. First, it incorporates the most recent historical and archeological research from mainland China. Second, it eliminates the Ten Wings, or the bulk of the heavy-handed Confucian moralism. The result is a beautiful and streamlined oracle, whose predictive power is no longer smothered by "advice."

We recommend the Huang translation with only one reservation. We do not recommend the *I Ching* on a computer disk which is offered for sale on the back of the book. An *I Ching* on a computer disk produces hexagrams using a table of random numbers. This mathematical randomization will produce true answers based on chance probability, and that is not what we want from an effective mantic device. Instead, we recommend using the Huang translation in the following manner:

1. Use three Chinese coins.

2. As you shake the tumbler to produce the six lines, concentrate on the question.

3. Use a monotonous sonic input, such as a drumming tape or John Stannard's Energy Chime.

The use of a monotonous sonic input will induce the shamanic altered state of consciousness. This will tend to promote whatever precognitive abilities you many have. The results — over the long run — should be far better than anything explainable by randomness, chance, or probability. Needless to say, keep a detailed and dated record of every *I Ching* consultation; and when the expected outcome happens, or fails to happen, record the result with ruthless honesty.

Those who use the *I Ching* are faced with the unresolved problem of the relationship between the Hindu-Western elements and the Oriental elements. The latter are also a set of five, with deceptively similar names (e.g., Earth, Water, Fire), which on closer inspection turn out to be very different. See figure twenty-five.

—Figure Twenty-five—
The Oriental Elements

The center or fifth element is *Earth,* symbolized by the Ox or the Yellow Man (Smith and Wan-go-Weng, 1979: 76). What is the relationship between these five Oriental elements and the five Hindu-Western elements?

Hindu number symbolism associates the Hindu-Western elements with certain numbers:

One   =
Two   =   Water
Three =   Fire

```
Four  =  Earth
Five  =  (Siva)
Six   =  Air
Seven =
Eight =  (Visnu)
Nine  =
Ten   =
```

Danielou, 1985: 352-353

If these ten numbers are arranged in two columns, this produces pairs of numbers associated with elements. Each pair has a male (odd) and a female (even) number:

```
AIR    = 1 - 6
WATER  = 2 - 7
FIRE   = 3 - 8
EARTH  = 4 - 9
         5 - 10
```

Now, the first nine digits can be arranged in the magic square of 15, what the Hindus call the "All-Beneficent" Tantric Yantra:

		Fire		
	8	3	4	
Air	1	5	9	Earth
	6	7	2	
		Water		

Madhu Khanna, 1979: 157

When we turn to China, we find that the *Lo-Shu* or writing from the river Lo, is a magic square of 15. The number of the Tao is 15 (Ponce, 1970: 144-145). Furthermore, the Chinese elements are identified with numbers and cardinal points:

```
                          East
                          Wood

              8        3        4
      North                              South
      Water   1        5        9        Fire

              6        7        2

                          West
                          Metal
```

Saso, 1978: 138–140; Sherrill and Chu, 1983: 19

Hindu-Western Elements		Magic Square Number		Cardinal Point		Chinese Elements
Fire	=	3	=	East	=	Wood/Wind
Earth	=	9	=	South	=	Fire
Water	=	7	=	West	=	Metal
Air	=	1	=	North	=	Water
Aether	=	5	=	Center	=	Earth

—*Figure Twenty-six*—
Elements, Directions and Magic Squares

—Figure Twenty-seven—
The Dakini Arrangement
(Lama Chime Radha, 1981: 23)

The fact that the Hindu-Western elements are identified with specific numbers in the magic square of fifteen, and that the Oriental elements are also identified with specific numbers in the same magic square of 15 permits us to use this magic square as a translation device. See figure twenty-six.

That this translation is correct is confirmed by the Tibetan arrangement of the Dakinis, or female consorts of the Herukas (Negative or wrathful meditation Buddhas) as shown in figure twenty-seven.

Here the cardinal points have the expected Chinese elements and colors, but the *name* of each Dakini contains a reference to the corresponding Hindu-Western element. In the East, Vajra Dakini is the consort of Vajra Heruka, or the negative Lord of Fire. In the South, Ratna Dakini is the consort of Ratna Heruka, or the negative Lord of Earth. In the West, Padma Dakini is the consort of Padma Heruka, or the negative Lord of Water. In the North, Karma Dakini is the consort of Karma Heruka, or the negative Lord of Air (Trungpa, 1981: 79–80, 83–84, 104–105; Snellgrove, 1959: 93; Govinda, 1982: 205–208). This confirms that our translation of Hindu-Western elements, cardinal points, and Chinese elements, is correct. Furthermore, notice that, like the Hindus and Tibetans, the Chinese prefer a polar arrangement.

ON THE TAROT

The Tarot as a mantic or divinatory device, is used in two radically different ways:

1. Some Tarot readers, especially beginners, use the standard meanings of the cards (Butler, 1975: 109–192). This is like consulting a dictionary. It can be done by anyone. It requires little more than persistence, and a normal amount of interpersonal sensitivity. The results range from the trivial to the interesting, but they are never extraordinary. The reader is likely to use a layout or spread such as the Celtic Cross. A wise client should monitor how much advance information he or she gives the reader. The better type of reader will request no advance information, will do the reading, and will then ask the client whether or not this has answered his or her question. If the reader asks for the question in advance, then verbalize the question without giving your opinion or revealing your attitudes or expectations.

2. A few Tarot readers are clairvoyants. This is a matter of degree. At the limit, the cards are divested of their standard meanings and serve purely as a psychometric link between the client and the reader. If consulted by one client, a clairvoyant reader is also likely to use a layout

or spread. If reading for a group, the Tarot reader does not use a spread. The usual procedure is to have clients pick a card face down. The client alone knows the identity of his or her card. The selected cards are gathered, face down, and shuffled. The clairvoyant reader picks up the first card, identifies it, and begins to speak. The results of this kind of Tarot reading are often extraordinary.

PRACTICE SEVEN

How to Journey to the Upper World to Find a Teacher

Like the Lower World, the Upper World is made up of many levels, each with its own scenery and inhabitants. Some levels seem to be uninhabited, others contain crystals or brilliant lights. Some inhabitants are perceived as having a human form. Among these, one or more will be willing to become your teacher or guide. Teachers or guides are sources of information, wisdom, and problem solving. From a cross-cultural point of view, teachers or guides have the status of deities. Therefore, you never try to call them down to your level; you go up to visit them.

1. Journeys to the Upper World begin from a raised area: a mountain, a treetop, a cliff, a rainbow, a ladder, the world axis, or the world tree (Walsh, 1990: 148). We are going to use the roof of a house. Start with the preparatory technique by Glaskin described at the end of chapter two. Begin by massaging your feet and ankles, forehead and temples, and follow with the imaginal maneuvers that extend your feet and ankles and your neck and head. After you expand your aura, start the drumming tape (and the tape recorder) and visualize yourself standing on the roof of your house, facing East. Verbally, out loud, describe what you see. Turn clockwise to the South. Describe what you see. Turn clockwise to the West. Describe what you see. Turn clockwise to the North. Describe what you see.

Turn clockwise back to the East.

2. Call your power animal and say to it: "Please take me to the Upper World to find a teacher in human form." This request can be repeated as often as needed during the journey.

3. Together with your power animal, fly straight up. At first you will see clouds and space but soon you will pass through a kind of membrane (Walsh, 1990: 147). This passage is usually very easy. Should any difficulty appear here (or elsewhere), simply ask your power animal to push you, pull you, dissolve the obstacle, or whatever is needed. Remember to continue to describe your journey out loud.

4. After passing the membrane, you have entered the first level of the Upper World. Scan the domain looking for a man or woman or a being in human form. If you find no one, don't waste time. Remember, you are not a tourist, but someone engaged in a serious mission. Ask your power animal to take you straight up and go to the next level. Continue to scan for a being in human form.

5. As soon as you find a person, approach that person, and ask him or her: "Are you my teacher?" Ask the question two or three times. There are only three possibilities: a "NO" answer (verbal or in gesture), no answer, or a "YES" answer. If the person does not answer (or answers "NO"), thank the person, leave, go straight up to the next level. Once there, scan for a person and repeat the maneuver.

6. Eventually you will meet a person who answers "YES." Ask again to make absolutely sure that it is a "YES" answer. If in doubt, ask your power animal to confirm that this person is indeed your teacher. Then thank your teacher, and ask your teacher for his or her name. At this point you may want to hug your teacher, or express affection. By all means do so. Then visit and ask for advice.

7. At the end of your visit, thank your teacher, say good bye,

and ask your power animal to bring you back to your rooftop. Once you are back on the roof, thank your power animal and say good bye. Then seal the scene with a banishing pentagram.

How to Go Up to the God and the Goddess

In Chapter Six you were taught how to do a ceremony of ritual magic. If you have done it, you have discovered that it has some very positive side benefits. You have invoked the Watchtowers, or personified conscious intelligences of the elements. By doing this you have created a field of perfectly balanced energy. This field balances your energy. You usually perceive this as euphoria. In other words, a ceremony that invokes the Watchtowers has an automatic healing effect that tends to make up for any lack or deficiency which you may have in the areas of Earth, Water, Fire, Air, and Aether. Likewise, it tends to remove any excess. The ceremony balances the elements in the psyche of the participants.

But your ceremony is incomplete. You can use it to do effective magic, but you have no way of knowing whether the desired outcome will bring harm to you or to someone else. To remedy this you have to learn to raise your energy level to reach the realm of the Goddess and the God. This is done in the following manner:

a. You ask your Power Animal to take you on a journey to the Upper World to find the God and the Goddess. As you go up, you will notice that colors fade to pastels.

b. Ask your Power Animal to take you vertically through the colors of the rainbow—red, orange, yellow, green, blue, purple or indigo—and into the white light.

c. Once you reach the white light, expand your aura in all directions and try to merge with the white light. This will help you detach from your sense of ego, which is an obstacle in this endeavor.

d. At this point you are likely to see the God and the Goddess as gigantic figures.

e. Once you locate the God and the Goddess, ask for their assistance, to share in their energy and awareness, and to share in their experience. It is through that experience that one can learn everything.

f. Ask the Goddess and the God, "Will the magical operation that I am about to perform, bring harm to anyone?" This is very important because it is the only way to deal with the problem of unintended consequences. Your magical objective may not be possible; or it may be possible and bring great harm to yourself or to someone else. You need to recognize all the ramifications and consequences of your intended magical action. The answer, whether visual, auditory, intuitive, or in terms of feeling, may lead you to modify your magical objective or replace it with another target.

You can think of the Goddess and the God as archetypes of the collective unconscious. When you reach the white light, you are already in their domain, already inside their energy field. Whether you actually see them or not does not matter. If you do see them, say, as Greek deities, remember that this is a cultural projection. You cannot really see them as they really are. You see them in a form that is acceptable to your cultural assumptions.

The God and the Goddess are *not* versions of the God of monotheism. They are *not* omnipotent, omniscient, or responsible for everything in the universe (nothing is). They are not there to "forgive" you for anything and they do not expect you to grovel. These powerful archetypal energies are a source of wisdom and guidance. That is why we ask to share in their awareness and experience. Never forget that you can only perceive them through cultural projections. As love and nurturing, the Mother is life or *eros*. As lord of karma the Father is death or *thanatos*. These are the two fundamental concerns of humanity.

Have you noticed a striking similarity between the

shamanic procedure of journeying to the Upper World to find a teacher and the 20th century Craft procedure of journeying up into the white light to find the God and the Goddess? The similarity is not accidental. The Craft procedure seems to be a lineal descendant of the shamanic procedure, dating back to 11,000 B.C.E.

How do we communicate with power animals or archetypal deities? The problem is not in what you say to them, but in perceiving messages that they send to you. It has been suggested that we perceive feelings through the solar plexus, intuitions through the top of the head, images through the forehead and verbal messages through the temporal lobes on the sides of the head, one or two inches above each ear (Sanders, 1989: 20–37, 59–61, 88–95, 115–129). Our experience confirms that this is correct. Most of the replies from power animals and teachers will be in images or in silent verbal messages. We suggest that to perceive visual images you should focus your attention on the front of your head, behind your forehead. To perceive verbal messages, focus your attention on the temporal lobes, above your ears.

CHAPTER EIGHT

REMOVING SPIRIT INTRUSIONS & BRINGING BACK MISSING PARTS

The major techniques of shamanic healing involve manipulation of energy on the astral and etheric levels. In the empirical, natural world, the use of these techniques seems to work synchronistically, bypassing rational causality. Furthermore, these advanced techniques cannot be learned from a book. The reader interested in learning these techniques should contact The Foundation for Shamanic Studies (Box 670, Belden Station, Norwalk, Connecticut, 06852, U.S.A.) and make arrangements to participate in their experiential workshops.

Removing Spirit Intrusions:

The general procedure for removing spirit intrusions from a client's etheric body is well known and can be described in general terms.

1. The shaman uses drumming, rattling, and dancing to enter the shamanic state of consciousness.

2. In the shamanic state of consciousness, the shaman acquires what occultists call etheric vision. That is to say, he or she acquires the temporary ability to see into the etheric energy plane.

3. The shaman journeys into the client's tunnel, which we find in the Middle World, and locates parasitic intrusions. These are usually seen as large, repulsive insects, slimy snakes, or sludge.

4. The shaman scans the client, locates the spirit intrusion, and sucks it out of the client's body (Walsh, 1990: 101). It can also be removed by pulling it out with your hands.

5. The shaman spits out the intrusion into some neutralizing medium such as water (Harner, 1982: 156).

This technique involves some danger to the operator in that the shaman must be filled with power to avoid being invaded by the entity or entities extracted from the client. These entities are likely to be what the occultists call artificial elementals. Artificial elementals in the form of insects and snakes live in the Middle World or Lower Astral. Anger, rage, and fear produce an internal shift that opens and exposes a person to invasion by Lower Astral entities. Alcoholism and drug addiction do the same thing. That is why *delirium tremens* and drug withdrawal are often associated with visions and sensations of crawling bugs and snakes.

Angelique has had many years of experience in removing spirit intrusions. She has psychic vision and clairvoyant abilities. One tool that she uses to express these abilities is Tarot reading. Therefore, her practice of removing intrusions incorporates these modalities. What follows is an account of Angelique's technique:

There have been times when the client's tunnel seemed clear. My hands moving over the body did not find any energy distortions. Yet when I consulted the Tarot, it was apparent that something was hidden inside. Then I used the Tarot to find out where the intrusion was hidden in the body.

Once I know from the Tarot where the intrusion is located, I lay my hands on the area. I go to this place inside my being where there is silence and I sit waiting in that silence. The energy begins to build. Since I have called upon my power animals at the beginning, the sensation is as if I am inside one of my power animals and this energy is building inside of me.

I allow myself to become one with the client. I allow myself to feel what it feels like to be the client. At the same time, I stay power-filled. It is very important that you stay power-filled. At the time when you become one with the client, and begin to feel what your client feels like, if you are not power-filled you run the risk of acquiring or taking on this intrusion. Power-filled means being filled with the energy of your power animal who is there to protect you. By waiting and staying very calm I am able to experience all that is occurring and all that is hidden inside the client.

The moment I find what is hidden inside the client, a high pitched sound begins to emanate from my body. This high pitched sound resembles wind. It comes from me and seems to go through the client. I feel that this high pitched sound vibration comes out of my hands which are placed on the client's body. This sound is not made with my vocal cords. I experience it as a vibration in my body. This sound vibration shocks the hidden intrusion into leaving the client.

Sometimes I have seen black bugs flying out of someone's body, or the intrusion may look like black sludge or black energy. What is most hidden is likely to be an etheric vampire, an entity that sucks all the client's energy. So, when the intrusions leave, they usually fly out of the client's head or feet, or erupt like a geyser or volcano between my hands. I continue to wait. I continue to be one with the client. Because I am power-filled, my power begins to fill the client and the intrusions cannot stay inside. The high pitched sound chases the intrusions out of the client's body. At this point a Tarot card will verify that the client is clear and that no intrusions are left inside.

Sometimes, while doing acupuncture, it would be inappropriate to tell the client that he or she has an intrusion. In such cases, I put my hands on the client and allow the high pitched sound vibration to emanate. It is important to realize that ritual is not always necessary to accomplish results. On the one hand if your intention (meaning synchronized body, mind, and spirit) is aware and focused on the task at hand, ritual may not be necessary. On the other hand, until you are experienced in the process and understand the synchronized state, properly performed ritual will increase your chances of a successful outcome.

It is not unusual to find a death-wish in people who have cancer. I perceive a death wish as an impression or a knowing that at a deeper and perhaps unconscious level the person wants to die. Sometimes I find a death-wish in people who are or have been drug addicts or alcoholics. Often they will have a death-wish or sense of impending doom inside of them. When this death-wish is extracted from an alcoholic client, the extraction will have an effect on how the person reacts to drinking or not drinking.

I once saw a woman who drank heavily yet refused to admit that she had a problem with alcohol, although her family was aware of it. In doing an extraction, I found the normal infestations that afflict alcoholics, such as bugs and snakes from the Middle World. I also found a death-wish. The source of this death-wish was an energy vampire. She had acquired this intrusion from the Lower Astral or Middle World while in a drunken state or under the effect of drugs. The vampire had sucked out most of her energy and her energy field had turned black. In her ordinary consciousness, this woman reported that she felt physically fine. My power animals said that because of her death-wish, she would probably create a car accident or some other life threatening situation that could end her life in the near future.

What follows are a couple of examples from Angelique's practice:

Beth: female, age 24

I found a fanged snake in the client's tunnel. Inspecting the energy field over the client's body, I found a cool area in the upper back. The fanged snake was in the client's upper back. I removed the snake and neutralized it in water. After the extraction, the client said that she had had pain in her upper back for several years. The pain was gone, and has not returned.

Jeremy: male, age 25

Jeremy was a smoker who wanted to stop. In his tunnel I found dark areas with webs and spiders. I found spiders in the lungs and a dark cave with a snake in the solar plexus area. I sucked out the spiders and the snake and neutralized them in water. As I was removing the insects, I felt drugged. After the extraction, Jeremy told me that a few years earlier he had been a cocaine addict. I pointed out that a person is more vulnerable to get intrusions while under the influence of alcohol or drugs. Since the extraction, Jeremy has stopped smoking, and his lungs feel better.

BRINGING BACK MISSING PARTS

In acupuncture and other modes of Oriental energetic medicine, establishing a balanced and freely circulating life energy is the goal. With certain techniques you remove what is referred to as "evil" energy. It is also important to invigorate the "good" energy. If a person is deficient in this vital energy they are more vulnerable to external invasions of a pathological or problematic nature.

If you remove the alien and parasitic energy of an etheric intrusion, you must replace the loss by bringing back and reintegrating missing portions of the client's own vital energy. The general theory is that these portions are lost as a result of accident or trauma in the course of a lifetime. In 1976, Angelique developed a procedure for bringing back missing portions of a client's vital energy:

When I restore vital energy, my power animals take me to a huge golden hall. Inside this hall are millions of locked containers that resemble golden mail-boxes. This looks like an entire city of golden mailboxes. The hall has a gate-keeper, and sometimes the gate is closed. I stand before the gate-keeper and ask if I can find the lost vital energy of a certain person. The gate-keeper then opens the gates and takes me inside.

Before journeying to hunt for the missing energy, I will have identified the client by a distinctive piece of jewelry, hair, or clothing. I use this identification to find the right golden box. I open the box and either reach inside for the fragments, or they will jump out at me. Then a scene will begin to play. I see the traumatic scene that produced the loss of vital energy. Sometimes I do not see a scene. Whatever the details, I locate the energy fragments in the form of a light, a crystal, a box, or a replica of the client at an earlier age. These I bring back with me.

As I take the energy fragments from the golden hall to the gate, we go through the colors of the rainbow: violet, indigo, blue, green, yellow, orange, red. By the time the fragments have passed the red color they are clear, and any problems are gone. The fragment of vital energy may have been infested with an intrusion, and this intrusion needs to be removed before the fragment can be brought back to the client. The passage through the colors of the rainbow, automatically extracts the intrusion. Then I blow the energy fragments back into the client.

I have taught this procedure to a few others, and they have succeeded in reaching the city with the golden mail-boxes. There is a mailbox for every bundle of lost vital energy; it is a place of lost energy fragments.

What happens if the fragments refuse to return? This is quite common because the fragments are still locked into the memory of the intense trauma that produced the initial loss. So you talk to the energy fragment, or you have your power animals talk to it and try and convince it to return. Opinions differ about what to do if it still refuses to return.

Some neo-shamans hold that it is unethical to force the vital energy to come back. I differ from this view. Energy fragments do not understand what has occurred. You cannot argue rationally with a two year old or with someone who has been traumatized. Furthermore, I believe that the awareness, safety, life happiness, and completeness of my client is more important. So I force the energy fragments to come back. To do this, I will have my power animals get the fragments. Then I will trap the fragments inside the sound of a vibrating Tibetan bowl. There have been times when I have had to grab a fragment, bind it, and bring it back. Then, after blowing the fragment back inside the client, it is sometimes necessary to tie down the fragment with a gold thread until it has had a chance to reintegrate with the whole person, and recognize that it belongs there.

When a client asks for my help, it is my responsibility to do everything in my power to restore the missing balance in that client. Restoring the missing balance includes bringing back missing fragments of vital energy.

However, there have been times when my power animals will tell me to stop and return later because this fragment is not ready to come back. When this happens I may or may not see the missing fragment. Then I will go back to the client and explain that I need to see them again, because I was unable to bring everything back. During the next session I will journey to find and bring back the missing parts. I will ask my power animals whether something is still missing, and continue to restore vital energy until the client is whole and harmoniously balanced.

If an energy fragment does not want to come back because the client is in a coma or wants to die, I ask my power animals what to do and trust what they say. Lost fragments are confused and refuse to return because of the pain of the original trauma. Therefore, you cannot trust what a fragment tells you.

My power animals have access to higher wisdom than the trauma-filled fragment. If my power animals say bring it back, then I will force it to come back. If my power animals say that it is time for this person to die, then I would not interfere.

After I bring the energy fragments back to the client I have the client do an inner journey to visit the retrieved fragments. While this is going on I play the Tibetan bowl. This is my innovation. I have found that the sound of the vibrating Tibetan bowl activates spirit memory and helps the client to reintegrate. I have also found that this sound cleanses any trauma from the fragment so that it is not disruptive when returned to the client.

Here are some case histories from Angelique's practice:

Bob: male, age 30

An auto accident broke Bob's back and left him a paraplegic. Acupuncture treatment produced considerable improvement. He left his wheel chair and began walking using two canes. At this point we decided to do an extraction.

As I entered his tunnel, I saw a scene from a past life in which many braves surrounded an old medicine man who was dying. One of the braves was Bob. The dying man asked to be buried with his medicine bag and his feather. The other braves left, and the dying man asked Bob not to take his feather. Bob promised, but took the feather as soon as the man died.

Now the spirit of the dead medicine man tells me that Bob cheated him in that life and continues to cheat women in this life. He adds that the accident happened to make Bob stop cheating people. Then Bob joined us, and we continued to talk in non-ordinary reality. Bob returned the feather and promised to stop cheating women. The medicine man accepted the feather and withdrew the curse. However, before leaving the tunnel, the medicine man said to me, "Bob will walk, but unless he totally stops cheating, he will not be free. Also, he will retain a limp as a reminder."

I obtained a power animal for Bob and told him about my vision in the tunnel and my conversation with the medicine man. Bob admitted the cheating and promised to reform. At this point my husband arrived and Bob got up to go to the rest room. My husband asked Bob, "How long have you been walking without canes?" As Bob realized what he was doing, he quickly grabbed one cane.

Bob left the area, and I saw him a year later. He was still walking with one cane. He had not totally quit cheating, but he was working at it with the help of a psychologist.

Mary: female, age 35

This woman came to me with a complaint about her eyes. In her tunnel, I found her body to be full of roots, foliage, branches and earth worms. I sucked all that out with a crystal. I then asked my vulture to devour whatever was left or hidden from sight. I obtained a power animal for Mary. Then I restored vital energy. My guides took me to the Golden Hall of many boxes. I opened a box, and found it to be full of beautiful eyes in various shapes and colors: yellow, blue, green, and brown. In the middle of the eyes was Mary's energy fragment. I asked it to come back with me, but it was reluctant because it felt that Mary was in danger. I told it that Mary was no longer in danger and the fragment agreed to return.

As I told Mary about the journey, she revealed that the illness afflicting her eyes had developed because her father and then her first husband abused her by punching her in the eyes. It seemed that her energy fragment had fled and sought refuge among healthy eyes. Furthermore, Mary was used to taking on everyone else's problems. She was a kind of mother earth, taking on the problems of the world. These appeared as the roots, foliage, and earth worms inside her tunnel. We talked about how to stop taking on other people's problems. It turned out that Mary also had a drinking problem.

As a result of removing spirit intrusions and restoring vital energy, her eyes have improved. So has her psychic vision. She has stopped drinking and is now in Alcoholics Anonymous.

Tim: male, age 11

Tim's parents brought him to me for acupuncture to help with his learning disability. He was functioning at kindergarten level while in the fifth grade. Unlike normal children who could ride a bike to school, Tim and other handicapped children had to ride the bus. Tim's mother believed that there had to be "something" that would help Tim be normal. Acupuncture treatment made a big difference. Tim calmed down, learned to concentrate and to handle abstract thoughts, and his grades improved. At this point, Tim's mother and I discussed shamanism, and she urged me to remove spirit intrusions and restore his vital energy.

In Tim's tunnel, I found him disconnected and levitating above his physical body. In addition, he seemed to have the spirits of a dead man and a crazy little boy. I extracted these entities. Then I found Tim's energy fragments, brought them back, and wrapped his astral and physical bodies with a gold cord. I then brought him a power animal.

After these procedures, Tim's mother explained that when Tim was age four, the family moved into a house where Tim slept in the same room which had been occupied by a little boy from a previous family. That little boy was autistic and had died of a brain tumor. She said that Tim's hyperactivity, low attention span, and other problems, had started about this time.

The morning after the removal of intrusions and restoration of vital energy, Tim astounded his mother by getting dressed by himself, putting on his shoes, gathering his books, and coming down stairs for breakfast. They lived in a five-level house, and the mother was used to finding shoes on one floor, clothes on another, and books on another. Before acupuncture, she had had to force him to get up, and help him to dress. Before the removal of intrusions and restoration of vital energy he had been unable to put on his shoes and gather his books by himself. After the removal of intrusions and restoration of vital energy Tim won an award at the Science Fair, was doing well in sixth grade, and was considered to be functioning normally.

John: male, age 35

In the tunnel of this man I saw the story of a past life being played out. He was with a woman and they were much in love. They pledged to love each other for that lifetime and for all eternity. The woman drowned, and the man was unable to save her. The man mourned her death and died of grief. I saw the man being reborn as my client John, and the energy of the woman came along with him. [In this lifetime, John has had a difficult time finding a "perfect love" or making a commitment].

The scene changed to the present, but still in the inner planes. The woman led John to a bridge. I often see this bridge when I am doing psychopomp work and escorting a dead person to their destination. At this point I realized that John is considering suicide. He wanted to die because he unconsciously wanted to be with his ghostly love. I talked to both of them and explained to the woman that she is destroying his life. This bondage is not necessary because they can meet again. They refused to listen. My power animals said that I must stop him. My guides told me to scream in his ear. I did so very loudly in ordinary reality. In the inner planes, he turned away from the bridge and let go of the woman. She stepped on the bridge, and before he can turn back towards her, both woman and bridge disappeared. After the journey, I blew John's energy fragments into his chest and into the top of his head.

Afterwards, John acknowledged that he had been feeling very lonely and overwhelmed by emptiness. He said that he had planned to commit suicide right after his session with me. His suicidal feelings are now gone, and his life has changed. It is interesting to note that while I was working on John, his body (in ordinary reality) was shaking and moving about on the floor. However, John had no awareness of this. He reported that he had heard me calling him from far off when in fact I was literally screaming in his ear as loudly as I could. My sense is that I would have lost John had I not screamed in his ear. It is important to follow the directions given by your power animals.

Alice: female, age 35

In her tunnel, I found a death wish and a snake coiled in her uterus. Her death wish was self-created, so I talked to her spirit and she agreed to release it. I removed the snake by sucking and pulling, and then neutralized it in water. Then I brought a power animal to the client and went on to restore her vital energy. The energy fragment appeared as a little girl who had left because she was not loved. I brought this fragment back to the client.

Alice confirmed the death wish. She said that as a child, her parents told her that they did not love her or want her. Later on, she had cervical cancer which was treated successfully by Allopathic medicine. The medical intervention removed the cancer, but did not correct the energy imbalance, and this allowed the snake intrusion into the area of her uterus.

Anthony: male, late 30's

Anthony and his wife had been trying to conceive a child for the last five years. Medical tests showed that Anthony had a zero sperm count.

In Anthony's tunnel, I encountered a past life scene. An Indian brave was dying with a curse that he would have no children. The curse came from another tribe. The brave was buried under an eagle cape to keep the curse alive. In the inner planes, a ritual was carried out, involving myself, the Indian brave, and members of the other tribe. In the ritual, I used my higher guide and my power animals to remove the curse. This involved the use of water and of colored lights.

Next I saw an Indian in full feather headdress, and a white aura around him. He came from the sky, went through water, and reached a clear area where there was a human skeleton. The Indian lay down on the bones and then rose up to indicate that the spirit of the bones was now free.

I extracted a coiled snake from Anthony's lower abdomen. The Indian brave, who had been under a curse, was Anthony's lost energy fragment. This was brought back and blown into his chest and head. I discussed what had happened, and Anthony said he had been having dreams of an Indian doing the "Bear Spirit" dance. He also saw water and colored lights. Two days later, Anthony and his wife conceived their first child.

The status of past life visions remains problematic, and I make no claims about them. I see a "story" associated with an energy blockage in the body of a client. I treat the story "as if" it were objectively real, for it *is* real in the inner planes. I remove the blockage or correct the energy imbalance, and results follow in ordinary reality. These procedures are similar to those in Oriental Energetic Medicine, where you balance the energy system by making up a deficiency or by removing an excess.

CHAPTER NINE

PAST LIVES,
THE TRAUMA OF BIRTH,
THE ENCOUNTER
WITH DEATH

I, George, discovered how to do past-life regression using a shamanic framework. Using shamanism has some advantages over all other past-life regression procedures:

1. The presence of your power animal protects you;

2. Your power animal has all the missing information, so all you have to do is turn to your power animal and ask (e.g., What year is this?).

Sometimes the power animal will refuse to take you to visit a past life. This means that the power animal is protecting you from emotional overload or protecting you from information which you cannot handle successfully at this time. This happens rarely, but if it happens, accept it and try again later.

The investigation of past lives is not a game, nor an object of idle curiosity. On the contrary, it is hard work often associated with suffering and stress. The reason for this is obvious. Great happiness, extraordinary good luck, great talent, great beauty, great wealth or great power are available to only a small fraction of humanity. The rest of us lead insignificant lives, unrecorded by history.

So, if past lives are often stressful or banal, why should we bother? The short answer is that the wise occultist will want to use visionary experience to resolve and dissolve as much past karma as possible. The long answer is that past lives exhibit patterns of feeling and behavior which are also present in this lifetime, and make a sizable contribution to our current failures and frustrations. If we can use visionary experience to relive those traumas in their past life setting, and then let go of the negative affect, we attain a measure of liberation. In the end both answers are the same.

Considered in an extended framework, past life identities are our own secondary personalities. To acknowledge them and accept them as our own is part of the process of integrating what Jung called the shadow. Eventually we recognize that everyone we dislike or hate, in this life or in a past life, is disliked or hated because they carry projections of our own unacknowledged and rejected impulses.

The ontological status of past lives remains controversial. Most Western occultists subscribe to a 19th century evolutionist or progressive theory of reincarnation. Hindus and Buddhists see reincarnation as the unfortunate result of ignorance, attachment and delusion—a horizontal and circular voyage that goes nowhere. Alternatively, you may be more comfortable with the idea that past lives are memories stored in the Jungian collective unconscious. It really does not matter whether you believe in reincarnation. You are welcome to view the whole subject of past lives as the projection of secondary personalities (Woolger, 1988: 39–77). What matters is not the belief but the visionary experience.

If handled with ruthless honesty, the ability to do shamanic past-life regression by yourself, to yourself, can be used as an effective technique of self-therapy. Regardless of the ontological status of past-life memories, this technique enables you to objectify, examine and change current life-patterns that may be victimizing you. For this reason, it is unwise to go along with those therapists who treat past-life memories as fantasies and suggest that you fantasize alternative and "happier" outcomes. The therapeutic power of past-life memories depends on our ability to respect the integrity of those memories. Criminal or sadistic behavior in past-life memories points to the current existence of those impulses in one or more of our alternative selves. This must be faced, before it can be controlled or modified.

The records of past lives are located in the Middle World. To tap them you need to journey with your power animal and use a horizontal tunnel. To produce the dissociation peculiar to the shamanic trance you need to listen to a drumming tape through earphones and narrate your experience out loud as it happens. Arrange to tape record your narration and you will have a record of your journey.

The presence of your power animal will insure your complete safety. In addition, your power animal will provide information that may not be immediately available to you. For example, after you say to yourself out loud, "Who is your father? Describe him." You might be able to describe him but still not know his name. You then turn to your power animal and ask, "What is my father's name?" The same can be done to specify the year, and the place or country you are inhabiting. The recommended procedure is to get as much information as you can on your own, and then to ask your power animal to fill in the missing details.

Throughout a past-life regression, and in order to enhance the dissociation of the shamanic trance, you will play two roles, both of which will be spoken out loud. In the first role you will ask yourself questions, and address yourself as "you." For example, "Describe your surroundings" or "How old are you?" In the second role you will verbalize the answers. For example, "I see a brook and beyond that, a forest of pine trees" or "I am 25 years old."

To enter the Middle World you need to visualize a *horizontal* tunnel. This tunnel should start from a feature in ordinary reality such as the front door of a familiar house (Wagner McClain, 1986: 42) or an actual physical cave. The reason for this is the need to maintain a clear boundary between ordinary reality and shamanic reality. The Middle World begins at the point where you enter that cave or open that door. Your tunnel is going to be visualized as glowing with the primary colors of the spectrum. For a journey into the past, these should be strong, primary colors (the opposite of pastels). Right behind the door will begin the red zone, then orange, yellow, green, blue and finally purple. After the purple zone, the tunnel ends in brilliant white light.

The experience of linear, irreversible time is largely confined to the ordinary world and to ordinary consciousness. Freud and Jung agreed that the unconscious has no sense of time (Woolger, 1988: 118). Linear, irreversible time does not exist in the Upper, Lower or Middle World. This means that in the Middle World the memories of past lives are arranged side by side, not in a sequential or linear fashion. Remote past lives and recent past lives are equally and immediately accessible. Each of us is an aggregate, and only a portion of that aggregate incarnates at a given time.

SHAMANIC PAST-LIFE REGRESSION

To do shamanic past-life regression you begin with the Glaskin procedure which you were taught at the end of chapter two. However, this time you end with the expansion of your aura and do *not* visualize yourself standing on the roof of your house.

1. Begin by massaging your feet and ankles for three minutes. Next, make a fist and massage your forehead in a circular motion for two minutes, then your temples in a circular motion for two minutes. Mentally extend your feet

and ankles for two inches, then extend your head and neck for two inches. Mentally move back to your feet and ankles and extend them 12 inches. Follow by extending your head and neck to 12 inches. Then extend your feet and ankles to 48 inches, followed by extending your head and neck to 48 inches. Now, enlarge your energy field until the front edge touches the ceiling.

2. Put on your earphones with a drumming tape. Turn on your tape recording equipment.

3. Next, mentally stand in front of your selected house, and describe what you see (out loud). Mentally change to the next season, and describe what you see. Repeat this mental change to the next season, describing what you see, twice more. You have now examined the changes in the front of this house through spring and summer, fall and winter. Return to the initial season (Wagner McClain, 1986: 41-42).

4. Mentally stand in front of the front door of the house. Visualize that a long, *horizontal* tunnel extends behind the door of the house. The first part of the tunnel is red, then orange, yellow, green, blue and finally purple. After the purple zone, the tunnel ends in brilliant white light. Open the door and describe the tunnel (out loud).

5. Call your power animal. Ask your power animal (out loud): "Please take me back in time to visit a past life that is most significant for understanding this life as _____ [your name]" or "Please take me back in time to visit the past life I lived before this one."

6. Narrate out loud as both of you move through the various zones of the tunnel and into the white light. Some where in the white light you will come to a stop. Now get ready to ask questions out loud and to provide answers out loud.

7. Look at your feet and legs—what are you wearing? Look at your hands—what is the color of your skin? Are you male or female? How old are you? What is your name? What year is this? Describe your surroundings. What place or country is this? Who is your father? What is his name? Describe him. How do you feel toward him? Who is your mother? What is her name? Describe her. How do you feel toward her? Do you have any brothers or sisters? Do you love anyone? Are you happy? What do you do everyday? (Wagner McClain, 1986: 43-44). If you have difficulty getting answers to any of these questions, ask your power animal.

8. Ask your power animal (out loud): "Please help me scan forward over the next 10 years." Where are you? What has happened in your life?

9. Ask your power animal: "How many more years are left before my death in this lifetime?"

10. If you still have one or more decades, then repeat item 8 as needed. Scan the events of that lifetime in decade units and report out loud everything that happens.

11. Ask your power animal: "Please take me to the day of my death and show me how it happens." Describe it in detail out loud. Pay particular attention to whatever happens to you after death.

12. After going through the death experience, ask your power animal: "What is the significance of this past lifetime for my present lifetime?" Describe it in detail out loud.

13. Ask your power animal (out loud): "Please take me back to my present lifetime." You will return to the white light and re-enter the tunnel, starting with the purple zone. When you reach the red zone, open the door, exit, and close the door behind you. Then seal the door with a banishing pentagram of white light. Thank your power animal and say good bye.

Some Case Histories

Nathan: male, age 30

Nathan is highly educated. He is Jewish, but not a religious believer. He works part of the year with a fishing fleet, and devotes the rest of his time to cultural pursuits and the martial arts. He is very unhappy. He feels disconnected from life, and he seems unable to form stable relationships with women. He is very attached to his mother and very concerned with not becoming a copy of his father. He does not want to follow in his father's footsteps. His father is a successful New York art dealer.

Nathan's power animal is a panther. In the following excerpts from a past-life regression he discovers that he lived as a 16th century Moslem.

Q: Look at your feet and legs, what are you wearing?

A: "I am dressed in some crazy clothes: circus clothes, or court clothes, or Turkish. My legs are covered with very colorful clothing: black, gold, red. Balloon like pants down to below the knee. I am wearing a vest."

Q: What year is this?
A: "1582."

Q: How old are you?
A: "Forty."

Q: Ask panther to show you your father.

A: "He has a sharp pointed beard, Arabic style. He is very wealthy. He is some kind of government official. He is some kind of Feudal lord or something."

Q: How do you feel toward your father?

A: "I feel like a lot is required of me, like a test. Mixed feelings. Anger, indifference. Indifference born of anger. Fear."

Q: Ask panther to show you your mother.

A: "She is wearing lavender blue. She is very Middle Eastern, Mediterranean looking. She is very beautiful. She has a kind of warmth and strength about her."

Q: What are your feelings toward your mother?
A: "Enormous love, closeness, support. I feel that she is stronger than my father."

Q: Ask panther what country are you in?
A: "Persia or Turkey."

Q: Which one?"
A: "They are the same." [Note: In the 16th and 17th centuries, the western portion of Persia and all of Turkey were part of the Ottoman empire]

Q: Do you love anyone?
A: "I don't know. I feel very alone. I only love my mother."

Q: Ask the panther to help you scan forward over the next 10 years, to age 50. What has happened?
A: "I feel bored and sad. I feel disconnected [deep sighs and tears]. I am sitting in a chair, looking at plants and flowers. I am doing my father's job."

Q: What happened to your father?
A: "He is retired. He is old, grey, and frail."

Q: Where is your mother?
A: "She is next to me or nearby."

Q: Do you love anyone besides your mother?
A: "I loved someone, but she is physically gone. I have lost someone."

Q: Are you happy?
A: "No. I feel like I am just pacing out time, being detached, looking."

Q: Ask panther to take you to scan the next 10 years, to age 60. What has happened?
A: "Now there is a young woman. Dark hair, light complexion. She is in her late 20s."

Q: How do you feel toward this woman?

A: "A great deal of love and warmth, even gratitude. We have children. I still feel kind of detached toward her because I am older, almost fatherly."

Q: Does your wife love you?

A: "Yes."

Q: Are you happy?

A: "Yes. I feel like I am involved, connected. I love holding my children, and feeling their soft flesh on mine. I love to watch them play."

Q: What has happened to your father and mother?

A: "My father died. My mother is also dead." [Note: Nathan was happy during the last two decades of his life. He was completely focused on his wife and children, and indifferent to his job as a government official].

Q: Ask panther to take you to witness your death.

A: "I am in a large bed, sheets, pillows. I am very old. My breathing is very shallow. Down at the left foot of my bed, I see my son pacing. I see my wife. I feel how close we have grown. She is standing beside me. I feel her hands on my arm. She smiles. She is still pretty, but she is older. She has crows feet.... I sink into myself. I feel pain for her. She is crying. I am floating above my body. It is very dark."

Q: Ask panther, what is the significance of this lifetime for my present lifetime as Nathan?

A: "Panther says that I don't feel connected because I am not connected to someone. I am not taking part in the big cycle."

Comment:

In a lifetime as a wealthy Moslem, Nathan did follow in his father's footsteps as a government official. His excessive attachment to his mother resulted in his being unable to establish successful relations with other women. This pro-

duced great unhappiness and a feeling of being disconnected. Finally, in late middle age, following his mother's
death, he married a much younger woman and had children.
He enjoyed a couple of decades of happiness. So far, Nathan's
life as a Jewish-American has mirrored the patterns of his
past life as a 16th century Moslem.

Sandra: female, age 36

Sandra has been married several times and is now
divorced. She has worked at various secretarial and adminis-
trative jobs. She always wanted to have children, but an early
hysterectomy made this impossible. She solved the problem
by adopting a baby girl. In the last year, Sandra has begun to
study holistic healing, and has completed training as a certi-
fied massage therapist.

Sandra's power animal is an eagle. In the following
excerpts from a past-life journey, she discovers that she lived
in the 17th century as a female Native American.

Q: Look at your feet and legs, what are you wearing?
A: "My feet are bare. They are brown. I am wearing
leather buckskin. I am an Indian woman. I have leather and
beadwork on my arms."

Q: What year is this?
A: "1597."

Q: How old are you?
A: "Twelve."

Q: Ask your eagle, what tribe do you belong to?
A: "Crow."

Q: Who is your father? Describe him.
A: "My father has long black hair. His face is painted
black and white in halves, with red lines on it. He is wearing
his warrior garments. He is dressed for a hunt."

Q: Who is your mother?
A: "My mother is dead. Her name was Sunrise."

Q: How do you feel toward your father?

A: "He frightens me. Since my mother's death he has been filled with grief. He is very angry."

Q: Do you love anyone?

A: "I love my brother, Raven Wing. He is 18 years old and coming into his manhood. He has taken his place among the warriors. He is very strong. I sense a lot of sadness. He is going to be leaving to get his new bride, in another camp, two days away. And I know that it won't be the same when he comes back."

Q: Ask your eagle to help you scan forward over the next 10 years, to age 22. What has happened?

A: "We are out on an open plain of grass, following a herd of bison. I am now married."

Q: Describe your husband.

A: "He is short and stocky. He has nice features but is not striking in any way. He looks kind."

Q: What are your feelings toward him?

A: "Respectful. He doesn't mistreat me in any way, unlike some of the other men with their wives. He has rounded cheeks. When he smiles his whole face lights up. He takes good care of me."

Q: Do you love anyone?
A: "No."

Q: Are you happy?

A: "I don't feel happiness. I am not able to have children. That has caused grief to my husband. So he is going to take on another wife."

Q: How do you feel about that?

A: "A man needs to have children. I feel that I have failed him."

Q: Ask your eagle to help you scan over the next 10 years, to age 32. What has happened?

A: "I am sitting under an overhang up on the side of a mountain. There are patches of snow on the ground. The second wife is with me, and one of her children."

Q: How do you feel toward her?
A: "She is very pleasant. She works hard. We don't fight. She accepts me. We have become close."

Q: How do you feel toward your husband?
A: "He is a good man, but I don't have much feeling for him. It hasn't changed. He is happier now that he has children, and so he lets me do the things I want to do."

Q: Are you happier now?
A: "I am resigned to life as it is. It is nice to have children around. But it is still painful knowing that I wasn't able to complete the honor of my family."

Q: Ask your eagle how many years you have left before your death.
A: "Six."

Q: Ask your eagle to take you to witness your death.
A: "I am laying on a skin. I am covered with splotches, all over me. I have a fever. I am having visions. I see the spirit world. I am calling to my ancestors to take me from here. The medicine man is burning sweet grass. He wears a buffalo head ... We are in the round house. The medicine man leaves. The fire is dying down. I feel very light. I look down at my body laying there, and I don't have any feelings about it."

Q: Ask your eagle, what is the significance of this lifetime for your present life as Sandra?
A: "I came into this life [as Sandra] with a great thirst for having children. And again, I was not able to have one. And again, I took a different option this time [adoption]. And I have come to terms with motherhood, which I never did in the past lifetime. Eagle says that my last years were spent working with the medicine man, which is how I became ill. The village came down with a sickness. Working with differ-

ent people, I too became sick and died. Now [in this life as Sandra] I am bringing back those energies. It has a lot to do with the path I am presently choosing to follow in the medicine way. That was the most recent lifetime in which I did healing work and called on the powers of the animals, the trees, and the flowers. Eagle says that that is my path in this lifetime."

Comment:

Once again, Sandra's past lifetime and her present lifetime share major patterns: the desire to have children and the inability to do so; a healing vocation.

After a few past-life journeys, you will find out that the behavior of a lifetime seems to produce a pattern which extends beyond physical death. It seems to determine your selection of parents for your next incarnation. For example, if you have behaved like a sadistic bully this pattern determines that you will be born the helpless offspring of sadistic bullies. This reveals that there is more justice in the universe than we had previously thought possible.

In turn, this enables us to go beyond the unqualified pessimism of the ancient Gnostics. That injustice rules the world is still true, but only if you have never investigated your previous incarnations. This insight should give no one an excuse for complacency or for justifying the status quo. The whole point of reincarnation seems to be the gradual elimination of oppressor and exploiter roles, and the gradual reduction of the sum total of human suffering.

Eventually, the investigation of past lives yields the experiential discovery that each one of us has been everyone else. If we have been everyone else, then, in a sense, we *are* everyone else. The gap between selfishness and altruism closes. You strive to treat the other as yourself because the other *is* yourself. In this manner, an ethic based on positive reciprocity acquires a foundation in experiential reality.

THE TRAUMA OF BIRTH

The work of Stanislav Grof (see chapter two) has shown that birth trauma experiences are associated with adult neurotic problems. While not as intense as Grof's LSD psychotherapy or his holotropic therapy, shamanic past-life regression allows you to access knowledge of birth trauma experiences in a protected framework.

Up to a point, the technique is identical to the one for past-life regression. You call your power animal, you open the door, and you gaze into your dark, horizontal tunnel with its bands of primary colors: red, orange, yellow, green, blue, purple, and the white light. You say to your power animal, "Please take me back in time to scan my prenatal experience. Take me to the moment before the start of labor in my mother's womb. Help me to witness and feel my birth experience." Then both of you move along the tunnel until you come to a stop somewhere in the white light.

Michelle: female, age 29

Q: How does your body feel?
A: "Hot."

Q: Scan the sensations of your body.
A: "My head feels pinched together. My legs and arms are curled up around me."

Q: What is it like outside your skin?
A: "Dark, warm, hard.

"I don't think I am going to like this.

"I am getting bumped all over the place. I am laying upside down from where I used to be. It is like there is an earthquake happening. I am being pressured. There is a lot of pressure. Everything feels really tight. What is going on here?"

Q: Scan your feelings.
A: "I feel scared. But I think it is the woman who is scared. I can hear her crying. I know it is not me. I still feel

safe and warm, except that everything is really tight. I am getting dizzy now. It feels like I am spinning."

Q: Continue to scan your feelings.
A: "I am surrounded by anger."

Q: Is it *your* anger?
A: [Pause]. "Yes, it is my anger.

"I am really dizzy. I am spinning. Dizzy and angry. What a way to start off. I feel that I am rushing along very fast. I really don't want to go out there. Oh, no! Oh, no! Maybe it was the anesthetic. I am spinning really awful. Oh! I don't like this at all."

Q: Detach and just witness.
A: "Slowing down now. But I am cold all of a sudden. Moments of bright lights. I am still inside the womb. That must have been the passage of the last contraction. She is hollering a lot now.

"I feel numb. I am too tired to do this. Oh! my head hurts. Everything is so tight. Cold. Still angry and afraid.

"There is something really cold and hard under me. I feel rather sad but I don't know why. There are bright lights all around me. And there is this pain in my head. Nothing seems familiar."

Q: Ask your power animal to bring you back to the present moment.

Comment:

Michelle was raised to be passive, gentle, sweet, and to repress aggression. Notice how her birth trauma experience shows that she has difficulty acknowledging her own anger.

THE ENCOUNTER WITH DEATH

Immediately after physical death, the conscious spirit of a human or an animal finds itself in the Middle World.

This is not their proper destination, but only a temporary, half-way station. Human spirits belong somewhere in the light of the Upper World, in a zone where the living cannot enter. Animal spirits belong somewhere in the Lower World, and there too, the living cannot enter.

Due to a multitude of factors, human and animal spirits can become temporarily stuck, trapped or side-tracked in the Middle World. This has given rise to the famous world-wide role of the shaman as psychopomp or guide and helper of the dead. Over the last 20 years, Angelique has helped hundreds of dead people to go over into the light of the Upper World where they belong.

I learned this procedure from my guides. It began in my teens when one of my aunts died. At the funeral I heard a voice say "Angelique, I need your help going over." I had no idea what she was talking about. So I asked my guides and they explained.

I told my aunt that I would try to help her. In an inner journey my guides took me to meet my dead aunt. Together we went toward this beautiful, glorious light. My guides explained that sometimes, when people die, they need human energy to go into the light. I guided my aunt towards the light. This experience left me feeling drained of energy. Since then I have learned to do this without becoming depleted.

My guides explained that flowers at funerals serve a similar purpose. The dead use the energy from the flowers to go over into the light and pass beyond the Middle World. My guides said that because of this, living plants are much better than cut flowers. Also, the departed spirit will draw energy from the mourners. To pass into the light this energy is needed. I have clairvoyantly seen this happening at many funerals. This helps to explain why people feel so depleted after a funeral. Perhaps a celebration with singing, joy, and live flowers would be more useful for the passing spirit.

After my father died I found him standing in a doorway. He had one arm and one leg inside the light, waiting for me. I was very surprised. He said "I knew you would come."

I asked him "How did you know how to get here?"

He responded, "The things that you know, the things that you feel, are real. Keep trusting them." In that moment I realized that we had shared the same knowing, and then he said good bye.

To help the dead, you begin by going into your tunnel and calling your power animal to take you to the dead person. If you know the person, then you will be able to recognize them. If you are doing this for someone else, Joe's aunt Mary for example, then ask your power animal to take you to find Joe's aunt Mary. When you find her, you need to make sure that she knows that she is dead. Simply ask her, "Do you know that you are dead?" You want the person to acknowledge or recognize that they are dead. Then tell the person that you have come to help them to go into the light.

Many times they will go with you quite willingly. Some are looking for someone to help them go over. As an example, let's assume that someone died in a car accident. You may find that they are still living the accident. They don't understand that they are dead. As you approach the dead person, you may see the accident being repeated over and over. So you explain to them that they were in an accident and are now dead. The response will vary. Some respond as if they are going crazy: they scream, cry and may refuse to believe you. It is up to you and your power animal to help this person. Ask your power animal, "Should I stay with this person? Are there things that they still need to learn? Is there more for this person to experience? Should I force them to go into the light?" Your power animal will tell you what to do.

Sometimes your power animal will tell you that the person is not yet ready to go over. In that case, just leave and return to ordinary reality. Ask your power animal to let you know when the dead person is ready. You may return in three or four days and find that the dead person is in a different state, reliving parts of his or her life. Your power animal might tell you that the person is still not ready and needs more time. As soon as your power animal tells you that the dead person is ready, journey to meet the dead person and say, "It is now time to go over."

The entry point will appear as either brilliant, glowing, white light, or as a doorway into brilliant white light. Alternatively, it might appear as a bridge. This bridge looks like an arched Japanese bridge. As we approach the entry point the dead person might see relatives or loved ones who have passed on before them. Then the dead person enters the light and vanishes from view. You stay behind.

I have tried to follow across that bridge or tried to enter that doorway, but it is impossible — When I try, I find myself back in the tunnel or back in ordinary reality. We can only cross the entry point when we die. The living cannot enter.

Sometimes, when you journey to find someone who has died violently — for example, a homicide or a suicide— your power animal will take you to a region known as the *Land of the Dead*. It is a black and white domain, totally devoid of color. The dead don't belong here, but are temporarily trapped. They are in shock or compulsively reliving the traumatic circumstances of a violent death. The mood is sad, weary, mournful and unpleasant.

Eventually they will awaken by themselves and move on to the light where they belong. However, while in the Land of the Dead they need energy to awaken. This energy must come from a living human being or be provided by colors or by a quartz crystal. The black and white appearance of the Land of the Dead indicates this lack of energy.

If you journey to this domain to find someone who has died, you should bring along some colors (e.g., colored liquids or powders or a quartz crystal). When you enter the Land of the Dead you may feel that those trapped in it are trying to capture some of your energy. Your mission is to enter, recover the person, and leave. When you do this, it sometimes happens that other dead persons hook on to you. My power animal explains that this means that they are ready to go over. So you take them out of the land of the dead and into the light.

I disagree with those who argue that one should never

force a dead person to go into the light of the Upper World. I will do whatever my power animal tells me to do. I ask, "Should I take this person into the light?" If my power animal says "yes," then I take them over. If they resist, I hold on to them and push them toward the light.

Another option is to have your power animal talk to the dead person, and/or have your power animal help you to take the resisting person to the light. As soon as they get into the energy field of the light they stop resisting, and are instantly ready to go over. Some of these problems can be illustrated by case histories.

Case One

A friend of mine committed suicide. I journeyed to the Land of the Dead. Just before entering, I saw a crescent moon. So I became like the crescent moon and floated into the black and white region. The purpose of the disguise was to prevent other dead people from draining my energy. I found my friend, but could not get him to wake up and recognize me. I poured a sweet-smelling elixir into his mouth and he started to regain color. His light started to shine. Then I grabbed him, put him into my crescent moon, and together we floated in the direction of the light. We said good bye and he went over.

Case Two

Occasionally you might be asked by a client to find a person who died many years ago. You find them, and they are where they think they should be. The energy of the Middle World is fluid and plastic and responsive to our expectations. So a dead person stuck in the Middle World might shape the energy to look like what they expect heaven or paradise should look like. If they have done this, they may refuse to leave this illusion.

A woman asked me to find and help her father who had died in a fire 30 years ago. I asked my power animal to take me to him. I found a man who was digging in a beautiful little garden next to a miniature church. The church was empty. I said, "Do you know that you are dead?"

He said, "Yes."

I told him, "I have come to take you into the light."

He asked, "Why? I am already in heaven." I explained that he was not in heaven and he said, "But there is the church."

I responded, "That is an empty church. It is only an illusion that you created. You are not in the light. I can take you to the light where you belong."

He said, "No, I am where I belong." I informed him that his daughter had told me to come and find him. He said, "My daughter told me to go to the church, and that I would be O.K." I continued to explain that he needed to move into the light and that I had come to take him were he belonged. He finally agreed. As soon as he saw the light, he expressed great happiness, and thanked me profusely.

After I returned from the journey, I told the daughter what had happened. She stated, "My father was not at all religious."

I explained to her that her father had said that his daughter had told him, "Go to the church and you will be O.K."

Then she remembered that during the memorial service, she had placed her rosary on the ashes inside the coffin and she had prayed, "Please father, go to the church, the church will take care of you." And that is exactly what he did.

Depending on their religious beliefs, some people have an idea of what death or heaven should be like. That determines the illusory environment which they create for themselves in the Middle World.

Case Three

A friend of mine who was paralyzed and unable to walk, died. We had made prior arrangements for me to journey and help him to go into the light of the Upper World. When I found him, he wanted to run, walk, and play basketball. So we did that over the next three days. He also took the opportunity to visit some of the people he loved. Finally, during the funeral, he was ready to go over. However, he was held back by a lot of anger felt by some of the living. These people felt angry that he had died. This anger kept him attached to the Middle World. The more angry they felt, the more they held onto his energy. I was getting ready to force the issue and get him into the light despite the anger.

Then, during the funeral, a song was played, and the living let go of their anger. At that moment I closed my eyes, journeyed, and took him into the light. This incident made me realize that the intense feelings of the living can hold on to the spirit of someone dead. When someone dies, we need to release, and lovingly let them go.

Case Four

A Native American friend committed suicide. He believed that suicide was "sinful." When I journeyed to find him, he said, "I cannot go into the light until I am purged, because I killed myself."

I asked him, "How shall we purge you?"

He explained, "I have to go before the elders in the kiva, and they will purge me."

I asked my power animal to take us there. We entered a kiva. An elaborate ceremony followed. At first, the dead man lay flat on the floor. The elders used feathers and smoke and gave him herbs. There was also drumming. The spirit of the dead man began to float upwards and reached the opening at the top of the kiva. The elders said that he was ready to go over. Then I went to him and took him into the light.

Case Five

This last case is about myself. A few years ago I was hospitalized with pneumonia and almost died. I had a high fever for many days, and the doctors expected that I would not survive. I would die unless my spirit decided that it wanted or needed to stay among the living. For several days I felt the attraction of this beautiful, glowing light. This was the same light to which I had taken so many spirits of the dead.

In all previous times, I was not allowed to enter the

light. Attempts to do so resulted in my being back in my tunnel or snapping out of the trance into ordinary reality. This time it was different. I was floating into the light. I heard the singing of Gregorian chants. Indian drums were beating and other chanting filled the air. I was told that I could die if I wished and that it was all right to go into the light. From the light I was told that it was my choice to live or to die at this time. I was overwhelmed by a feeling of contentment, love and peace; my being felt like it was finally home. I was excited that I finally had the opportunity to choose whether to go or to stay.

When I spent longer periods in the light, my fever would go up. On same day that I decided to stay with the living, my fever broke and I started to recover. I left the hospital in a few days.

Being in the light was the most beautiful, most wonderful experience of my entire life. This experience has enhanced by ability to help the spirits of the dead. I now have a sense of what it feels like to enter the light of the Upper World.

Let us now summarize the shamanic procedure for helping the dead. The dead that need help are in the Middle World. Time, as we know it, does not exist in that domain. The belief and expectations of the dying structure what they will experience in the Middle World. Do not judge this. In all cases, ask your power animal what to do, and follow those instructions. Since those you want to reach are in the Middle World, you will need a *horizontal* tunnel, and you will need an appropriate entrance into that tunnel.

1. Journey into the Lower World, call your power animal, and ask, "Please show me an entry into the Middle World, which I can use to help the dead." The entry is likely to be something like a mandala, a rose window, a vortex or even a cave entrance on the side of a mountain. Return from your journey and draw your entrance in color.

2. Select your target: a dead person whom you would like to help.

3. Visualize your entrance on the horizon. Call your power animal and say, "Please take me to visit X."

4. Together with your power animal, fly into your entrance on a horizontal journey. Sometimes the dead person is already gone. Select an alternate dead person or ask your power animal to take you to a dead person who needs help.

5. As soon as you find the dead person, greet them and be recognized. Explain that they are dead. You may want to explain how they died. Then say, "I have come to take you to the light, where you belong."

6. At this point the spirit may have a message for someone living, or you may have a message for the spirit (e.g., something I wanted to tell my brother before he died).

7. If the spirit does not want to come with you, ask your power animal for advice. If the dead person needs more time, give him or her more time. If the power animal says that they are ready to go over, but they still refuse, then say to your power animal, "Please help me to take this person to where he or she belongs."

8. The entrance appears as one of three possibilities: a door way, a bridge or a burst of white light. A shaft of light may appear. Help the dead person to enter the shaft and send them straight up. Alternatively, a shaft of light may appear in the middle of the bridge. As soon as the dead person enters the light, they disappear.

9. Return from your journey and seal your entrance with a banishing pentagram of white light. Thank your power animal for its help.

ON HELPING ANIMAL SPIRITS

Between lives, animal spirits rejoin their group mind somewhere in the Lower World. However, those animals who possess unusual intelligence and a differentiated personality do not merge into the group mind. They retain their separate individual identity between incarnations.

After death, and exactly like humans, animal spirits experience a period of delay and confusion in the Middle World. This means that we can undertake a shamanic journey to find the animal and help it to reach its proper destination. The procedure is to visualize your entrance on the horizon, call your power animal, and together undertake a horizontal journey to the Middle World. You ask your power animal, "Please take me to find X (your pet's name)." What follows is an example from a personal experience by George, one of the authors of this book.

Background Information

I had my cat Inky for 13 years. He was a part-Siamese male, short hair, and all-black except for a white spot on his chest. We were very close. In winter, Inky would climb under the sheets, snuggle up, and go to sleep with me. He loved to sit on my chest and touch my face.

Inky was unusually intelligent. He would immediately respond to his name even if it was only mentioned in a casual conversation with someone else. He was neutered, and visited the veterinarian once a year to get his shots and have his teeth cleaned. About a year ago, Inky spent four weeks in the animal hospital and underwent two hours of open surgery to clear an obstruction in his bile duct, complicated by an infection. He survived the operation but never recovered his normal weight. Then the illness returned and he had to be put to sleep. After euthanasia, he was buried in the garden, below my wife's bedroom window.

Three days later I did a psychopomp journey. I asked my power animal, "Please take me to find my cat Inky." We flew into a purple vortex and came out into a dark zone. Suddenly, there he was in a small illuminated area. He seemed bewildered and kept probing the unfamiliar darkness around him. I asked myself, is this my cat Inky? This cat has the white spot on his chest, he has Inky's face, but he is several pounds heavier, and his black fur looks healthy and glossy. So I asked my power animal who confirmed that this is indeed Inky. At this point I noticed that Inky had recovered his testicles (once again, he is whole). Then Inky recognized me, and brought his dark luminous blue eyes and face close to mine.

I hugged him and kissed him. I explained that we love him but had to end his life to spare him more suffering and pain. I asked my power animal to repeat this explanation, and he did. Then I asked my power animal, "Help me escort Inky to wherever he is supposed to go."

The power animal answered, "You can only go with him part of the way." I lifted Inky on to my left shoulder and felt his fur against the side of my face. The three of us began a journey to the Lower World. We dropped straight down along an enormous steel-blue shaft (an Air version of the World Tree). We went past the levels which I usually visit and continued going down. I began to hear faint singing and music. Somehow, this told me that we were approaching our destination.

Suddenly, we reached a level and exited on to a dark rocky flat terrain. Ahead of us I saw a wide chasm. On the other side, about a block away, there were rolling hills in brown and orange. Suddenly, a tunnel-like bridge, made up of white light, appeared across the chasm. My power animal said, "He has to enter and go to the other side. That is the land of the cats. You cannot follow." I noticed that the diameter of the tunnel-like bridge was too small to allow a human to enter.

Inky was eager to get going. I said, "Inky, we love you so much. Come back to us when you can. Now go to the other side." Inky began to cross the bridge of light, and as he did so, the bridge disappeared behind him. My power animal said, "Look carefully, you can see him climbing on the other side. No, you cannot see the big cat, but he is there."

I asked, "Is Inky happy?"

The power animal said, "He will be."

At this point I saw this little black cat climbing on a diagonal over one of the orange-brown hills and disappearing over the top. I asked my power animal, "Is there anything else that we can do for Inky?"

My power animal said, "No." So we re-entered the steel-blue shaft and flew back up.

TO HELP THE DYING

While lacking external verification in ordinary reality, shamanic journeying to help the dead is a very comforting and healing activity. It helps counteract the feeling of powerlessness which is part of bereavement. Furthermore, it helps reduce the fear of death. This suggests that a modification of this technique may be of considerable use to the dying and the terminally ill.

I, George, stumbled upon this procedure in February of 1981, several years before encountering Michael Harner and his shamanic workshops. I was coming from four years of Jungian analysis, and as explained elsewhere, the Jungians do journeying under the name of active imagination. My mother was dying of terminal cancer. The increased fear of death brought about a reversion to the Catholic Christianity of her youth. I was visiting her, saying good bye, and desperately trying to help her. Fortunately mother was a good visualizer. I suggested trying a technique "that might show you what you are likely to encounter after you die." She was willing to try it.

1. I said, "Close your eyes and imagine the entrance to a cave on the side of a mountain. Let me know when you see it."

2. I said, "Describe the entrance and establish sensory awareness. Touch the walls. Smell the air. What is the ground like? Turn around and describe the scene behind you. Where is the sun? What time is it? Describe the weather."

3. I said, "Now, turn around and face the cave. It is the entrance to a horizontal tunnel. Start walking and let me know when you come out on the other side."

4. Mother reported that she came out into a garden with grass and flowers. Then she said, "Oh! Saint Francis!," and tears began rolling down her cheeks. She reported that she was on her knees and that Saint Francis of Assisi had placed a hand on her head.

5. I said, "Mother, ask Saint Francis to show you what you will encounter after you die."

6. She did so, and reported that Saint Francis took her on a path around a hill to the edge of a canyon. On the other side she could see a multitude which she recognized as her dead relatives. Among them were her beloved father, the grandmother who raised her, and her first born child who died before I was born. The latter was a little boy in short pants who was jumping up and down and waiving to her.

I guided mother through this journey on five consecutive days. Then I had to leave and return to another state. Later that year, mother died after spending a month and a half in a coma. Within hours after her death, Angelique journeyed to meet her, but the first journey was unproductive. Angelique reported that mother was slowly waking up. That evening, Angelique went back in and mother recognized her. Angelique took mother to the edge of a canyon, only now there was a bridge to go across. Angelique reported that as mother started on that bridge, a little boy in short pants came running to greet her.

It is clear that the fundamental rule to use when shamanic journeying to help the dying is to fully accept and adapt to their religious beliefs, or lack of thereof, in a nonjudgmental way. This is not the time to argue or to discuss religion. Furthermore, the dying person's religious beliefs may be such that it is impossible to teach them how to obtain a power animal. Consult your own power animal and ask for help. Then say to the dying person, "Would you like me to teach you a technique that might show you what you are likely to find after you die?" If they agree, ask them to visualize an entrance and guide them on a horizontal journey.

CHAPTER TEN

NEW
CHALLENGES

In a recent study of ritual magicians and Witchcraft covens in London, anthropologist T. M. Luhrmann found that modern magicians are sophisticated, well-educated, intellectual, middle-class people (Luhrmann, 1989: 7,10). Luhrmann became a member of Gerald Gardner's own coven, and she describes its social composition: the high priestess is a professional psychologist, the high priest is a computer software analyst. The membership includes a man with a degree in classics from Cambridge and a job at the Foreign Office, another Cambridge educated computer consultant, a woman teacher who was a former Oxford University lecturer, an electronics engineer, a woman photographer, a woman professional artist, a middle level manager of a large business, the manager of a large housing estate and a factory engineer (Luhrmann, 1989: 3, 21, 23, 30, 49). Another lodge of ritual magic included three civil servants, one university lecturer on computers, one computer software analyst, one homeopath, a therapist, a psychologist, a senior secretary at a major bank and another less senior, a nurse, a schoolteacher, two librarians, two actresses, a Borough Council employee, a graduate student, a mature woman student, an electrician, a retired woman and several mothers. The small group of ritual magicians led by Gareth Knight included a saddler, a teacher of subnormal children, a television actor who had been with the Royal Shakespeare Company, a builder, the headmaster of a comprehensive school, two students and a New York lawyer (Luhrmann, 1989: 66).

Luhrmann tried to understand why sane, successful, intellectual people are attracted to Witchcraft and ritual magic.

> *My findings suggest that the people who turn to modern magic are searching for powerful emotional and imaginative religious experience, but not for a religion per se ... magic does not require an explicit endorsement of a specific creed, or ... of a hypothesis of the divine at all ... The practice may promise spiritual enlightenment ... but it does so without violating an intellectual distrust of religious belief ... Magic has as much to do with the rejection of traditional religion as with its provision of religious experience."*
>
> Luhrmann, 1989: 337, 341

So modern Witchcraft and ritual magic provide religious *experience* without religious belief or faith. Here Luhrmann has successfully identified the visionary and experiential focus which links modern magic with ancient shamanism. This points to its increasing relevance for pragmatic, empirically-oriented, educated people in urban industrial society.

Throughout this book we have argued that shamanism is the source of the entire esoteric tradition, and that all magical practices will be enhanced when they are reintegrated within a shamanic framework. For a final example, consider sigil magic as developed from Agrippa and the medieval grimoires through the lifework of Austin Osman

Spare (1886 – 1956). This is a discipline which expresses the magical will in a sentence, transforms that sentence into a non-representational symbolic image or glyph called a sigil, then charges that sigil with power and sends it into the inner planes (or collective unconscious) to do its work. This procedure makes good sense because we know that the language of the inner planes is made up of images and not of abstract thoughts or words (Bardon, 1975: 79, 102). Furthermore, sigils are effective magical instruments for the magician who creates them and for no one else. In other words, each magician has to develop his or her own symbolic images to communicate successfully with the collective unconscious. How can shamanism improve on this? Shamanic procedures can improve the efficacy of sigil magic at two points: 1) in obtaining the sigils from the unconscious, and 2) in charging them with power.

In a very fine book on sigil magic, the contemporary German magician Frater U∴ D∴ has described the procedure for developing an alphabet of desire. This is a dictionary of symbolic images which a particular magician can use again and again in different combinations. The steps are as follows:

1. Formulate your magical will into a sentence. For example, "This is my will, to get top grades in the qualifying exam." You will need to obtain three sigils. The first for "This is my will," the second for "to get top grades" and the third for "in the qualifying exam."

2. Frater U∴ D∴ suggests using automatic writing to obtain these sigils from the unconscious (Frater U∴ D∴, 1990: 77–78). He points out that this laborious method requires time and patience, and that the first results are likely to be doodles or scribbles.

As a shamanic alternative we suggest the following. Enter the shamanic trance (by using a drumming tape or the John Stannard energy chime). Ask your power animal to show you the sigil that corresponds to each part of your magical sentence. This procedure takes a couple of minutes. Copy the three sigils as you receive them.

3. Let us pretend that you obtain the following three sigils:

This is my will

to get top grades

in the qualifying exam.

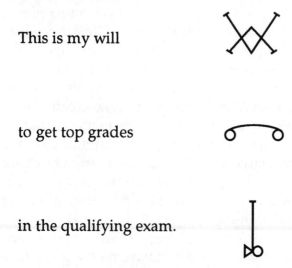

You then arrange these three sigils into a single sigil with a boundary or border:

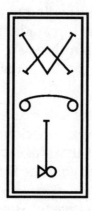

Now you are ready to charge your sigil with power.

4. Frater U∴ D∴ suggests charging the sigil by staring at it with an empty mind, while using the energy released by

sex magic or the Austin Osman Spare death posture (Frater U.∴ D.∴, 1990: 32–35).

As a shamanic alternative, we suggest that you re-enter the shamanic trance (using monotonous sonic input), stare at your sigil with an empty mind, and ask your power animal to charge it with power.

5. Release your sigil. To do this, inhale or absorb the sigil through your eyes (Frater U.∴ D.∴, 1990: 35), and shout.

6. Banish your sigil. Frater U.∴ D.∴ suggests using laughter. We suggest drawing a banishing pentagram. Now destroy the physical sigil by burning the paper. Then empty your mind and think of something else.

Try it. It works.

In the chapters of this book, we have examined portions of ancient shamanism and modern occultism and tried to separate fact from fiction, knowledge from superstition. Every recommended practice *is* recommended because we have tried it and found that it is indeed effective. If you, the reader, have tried out the various practices, then you have discovered what works for you and what you want to retain.

BIBLIOGRAPHY

Adler, Margot. 1986. *Drawing Down the Moon.* Boston: Beacon.

Bardon, Franz. 1981. *Initiation into Hermetics.* Wuppertal, W. Germany: Dieter Ruggeberg.

_____. 1975. *The Practice of Magical Evocation.* Wuppertal, W. Germany: Dieter Ruggeberg.

Basilov, V. N. 1984. "Chosen by the Spirits," pp. 3–48 in Marjorie Mandelstam Balzer ed. and trans. 1990. *Shamanism: Soviet Studies Of Traditional Religion in Siberia and Central Asia.* Armonk, New York: M. E. Sharpe, Inc.

Bradley, Donald A. 1973. *Solar and Lunar Returns.* St. Paul, MN: Llewellyn.

Brennan, J. H. 1971. *Astral Doorways.* New York: Samuel Weiser Inc.
Butler, Bill. 1975. *Dictionary of the Tarot.* New York: Schocken.

Cade, Maxwell C. and Nona Coxhead. 1989. *The Awakened Mind.* Longmead, Shaftesbury, Dorset: Element.

Campbell, Joseph. 1976. *Masks of God : Primitive Mythology.* New York: Penguin.

Carroll, Peter J. 1987. *Liber Null and Psychonaut.* York Beach, ME: Samuel Weiser Inc.

Castaneda, Carlos. 1974. *Tales of Power.* New York: Simon and Schuster.

Cheiro. 1929. *Palmistry for All.* New York: Putnam's.

_____. 1931. *You and Your Hand.* Garden City, NY: Doubleday.

Conze, Edward. 1975. *Buddhism : Its Essence and Development.* San Francisco: Harper and Row.

_____. 1975. *Further Buddhist Studies.* Oxford: Cassirer.

Danielou, Alain. 1985. *The Gods of India.* New York: Inner Traditions.

Denning, Melita and Osborne Phillips. 1980. *Psychic Self-Defense and Well-Being.* St. Paul, MN: Llewellyn.

_____. 1983. *The Magic of the Tarot.* St. Paul, MN: Llewellyn.

Dore, Gary, "The New Shamans" pp. 1–10 in *Newsletter of The Foundation for Shamanic Studies.* Vol.3, No.3, Winter 1990–91.

Eliade, Mircea. 1964. *Shamanism : Archaic Techniques of Ecstasy.* Princeton, NJ: Princeton Univ. Press.

Fagan, Cyril. 1962. *The Symbolism of the Constellations.* London: Moray Press.

_____. 1976. *The Solunars Handbook.* Tucson, AZ: Clancy.

Fagan, Cyril and Roy C. Firebrace. 1971. *Primer of Sidereal Astrology.* Isabella, MI: Littlejohn.

Furst, Peter T. "The Roots and Continuities of Shamanism," pp. 1–28 in Anne Trueblood Brodzky, Rose Danesewich, Nick Johnson, eds. 1977. *Stones, Bones, and Skin : Ritual and Shamanic Art*. Toronto: The Society for Art Publications.

Gauquelin, Francoise. 1982. *Psychology of the Planets*. San Diego, CA: Astro-Computing Services.

Gauquelin, Michel. 1988. *Written in the Stars*. Wellingborough, Northamptonshire: Aquarian.

Ginzburg, Carlo. 1991. *Ecstasies : Deciphering the Witches' Sabbath*. Trans. From Italian by Raymond Rosenthal. New York: Pantheon, Random House, Inc.

Glaskin, G. M. 1974. *Windows of the Mind*. San Leandro, CA: Prism.

Goodman, Felicitas D. 1988. *How About Demons?* Bloomington: Indiana Univ. Press.

_____. "Shamanic Trance Postures" pp. 53–61 in Gary Dore ed. 1988. *Shaman's Path*. Boston: Shambhala.

Govinda, Anagarika. 1981. *The Inner Structure of the I Ching*. New York: Wheelwright.

_____. 1982. *Foundations of Tibetan Mysticism*. York Beach, ME: Weiser.

Graves, Tom and Janet Hoult. 1980. *The Essential T.C. Lethbridge*. London: Routledge and Kegan Paul.

Grof, Stanislav. 1975. *Realms of the Human Unconscious*. New York: Viking.

_____. 1988. *The Adventure of Self-Discovery*. Albany, NY: SUNY press.

Guenther, Herbert. 1978. *The Life and Teaching of Naropa*. Oxford: Oxford Univ. Press.

Harner, Michael. 1982. *The Way of the Shaman*. New York: Harper and Row (Bantam).

_____. "Shamanic Counseling," pp. 179–187, in Gary Dore, ed. 1988. *Shaman's Path*. Boston: Shambhala.

_____. 1989. *The Foundation for Shamanic Studies Newsletter*. Norwalk, CT: Vol. 2, No. 2, p. 2.

Harrison, Michael. 1974. *The Roots of Witchcraft*. Secaucus, NJ: Citadel.

Howe, Ellic. 1972. *The Magicians of the Golden Dawn*. London: Routledge and Kegan Paul.

Huang, Kerson and Rosemary Huang. 1985. *I Ching*. New York: Workman Publishing.

Huizinga, J. 1954 [1924]. *The Waning of the Middle Ages*. Garden City, NY: Doubleday Anchor.

Kaplan, Aryeh, trans. and ed. 1979 [1170 A.D] *The Bahir*. York Beach, ME: Samuel Weiser Inc.

King, Francis. 1970. *The Rites of Modern Occult Magic*. New York: Macmillan.

King, Francis and Stephen Skinner. 1976. *Techniques of High Magic*. London: C. W. Daniel.

Khanna, Madhu. 1979. *Yantra*. New York: Thames and Hudson.

Lacarriere, Jacques. 1977. *The Gnostics.* New York: Dutton.

Lauf, Detlef Ingo. 1977. *Secret Doctrines of the Tibetan Books of the Dead.* Boulder, CO: Shambhala.

Laycock, Donald C. 1978. *The Complete Enochian Dictionary.* London: Askin Publishers.

Lewis, David "One Hundred and Eight Thousand Prostrations" pp. 203–205 in Don Monrreale ed. 1988. *Buddhist America.* Santa Fe, NM: John Muir.

Lurker, Manfred. 1980. *The Gods and Symbols of Ancient Egypt.* London: Thames and Hudson.

Luhrmann, T. M. 1989. *Persuasions of the Witch's Craft : Ritual Magic in Contemporary England.* Cambridge, MA: Harvard University Press.

Michaelsen, Scott. ed. 1989. *Portable Darkness : An Aleister Crowley Reader.* New York: Harmony Books, a division of Crown Publishers Inc.

Mumford, Jonn. 1988. *Ecstasy Through Tantra.* St. Paul, MN: Llewellyn.

Ophiel. 1972. *The Art and Practice of Getting Material Things Through Creative Visualization.* Los Angeles: Peach.

_____. 1972. *The Art and Practice of the Occult.* Los Angeles: Peach.

_____. 1976. *The Art and Practice of Caballa Magic.* Los Angeles: Peach.

Pagels, Elaine. 1981. *The Gnostic Gospels.* New York: Vintage.

Ponce, Charles. 1970. *The Nature of the I Ching.* New York: Award.

Radha, Chime, Lama Rimpoche, "Tibet," in Michael Lowe and Carmen Blacker, eds. 1981. *Oracles and Divination.* Boulder, CO: Shambhala.

Rawson, Phillip. 1978. *The Art of Tantra.* New York: Oxford Univ. Press.

Regardie, Israel. 1984. *The Complete Golden Dawn System of Magic.* Phoenix, AZ: Falcon.

Saso, Michael. 1978. *The Teachings of Taoist Master Chuang.* New Haven, CT: Yale Univ. Press.

Savage, Adrian. 1988. *An Introduction to Chaos Magic.* New York: Magickal Childe.

Scholem, Gershom G. 1941. *Major Trends in Jewish Mysticism.* New York: Schocken.

_____. 1969. *On the Kabbalah and Its Symbolism.* New York: Schocken.

_____. 1987 [1974] *Kabbalah.* New York: Dorset.

Shephard, John. 1985. *The Tarot Trumps.* Wellingborough, Northamptonshire: Aquarian.

Sherrill, W.A. and W.K. Chu. 1983. *An Anthology of the I Ching.* London: Routledge and Kegan Paul.

Smith, Bradley and Wan-go-Weng. 1979. *China : A History in Art.* New York: Doubleday.

Snellgrove, D. L. 1959. *The Hevajra Tantra. Vol.I.* London: Oxford Univ. Press.

Sperling, Simon, Levertoff, trans. 1934. [1270 A.D.] *The Zohar.* 5 vols. New York: Soncino Press.

Tart, Charles ed. 1972. *Altered States of Consciousness.* Garden City, NY: Doubleday Anchor.

Trungpa, Chogyam. 1981. *Journey Without Goal.* Boulder, CO: Prajna

U.'. D.'., Frater. 1990. *Practical Sigil Magic.* St. Paul, MN: Llewellyn.

_____. "Models of Magic," pp. 2–5, *Chaos International.* No. 9, 1990.

Valiente, Doreen. 1989. *The Rebirth of Witchcraft.* London: Robert Hale.

Von Franz, Marie-Louise. 1974. *Shadow and Evil in Fairy Tales.* Zurich: Spring.

Wagner McClain, Florence. 1986. *A Practical Guide to Past Life Regression.* St.Paul, MN: Llewellyn.

Walsh, Roger N. 1990. *The Spirit of Shamanism.* Los Angeles: Tarcher.

Westcott, Wynn W. 1975 [2nd century A.D.] *Sepher Yetzirah.* New York: Samuel Weiser, Inc.

Whincup, Greg. 1986. *Rediscovering the I Ching.* Garden City, NY: Doubleday.

Wirszubski, Chaim. 1989. *Pico della Mirandola's Encounter with Jewish Mysticism*. Cambridge: Harvard Univ. Press.

Woolger, Roger J. 1988. *Other Lives, Other Selves*. New York: Bantam.

Woodroffe, Sir John. 1981. *The World as Power*. Madras: Ganesh.

Yates, Frances A. 1969. *Giordano Bruno and the Hermetic Tradition*. New York: Vintage.

STAY IN TOUCH

On the following pages you will find listed, with their current prices, some of the books now available on related subjects. Your book dealer stocks most of these, and will stock new titles in the Llewellyn series as they become available. We urge your patronage.

However, to obtain our full catalog, to keep informed of new titles as they are released and to benefit from informative articles and helpful news, you are invited to write for our bi-monthly news magazine/catalog. A sample copy is free, and it will continue coming to you at no cost as long as you are an active mail customer. Or you may keep it coming for a full year with a donation of just $7.00 in U.S.A. & Canada ($20.00 overseas, first class mail). Many bookstores also have *The Llewellyn New Times* available to their customers. Ask for it.

Stay in touch! In *The Llewellyn New Times'* pages you will find news and reviews of new books, tapes and services, announcements of meetings and seminars, articles helpful to our readers, news of authors, advertising of products and services, special money-making opportunities, and much more.

The Llewellyn New Times
P.O. Box 64383, Dept. 325, St. Paul, MN 55164-0383, U.S.A.
* * *

TO ORDER BOOKS AND TAPES

If your book dealer does not have the books described on the following pages readily available, you may order them direct from the publisher by sending full price in U.S. funds, plus $3.00 for postage and handling for orders *under* $10.00; $4.00 for orders *over* $10.00. There are no postage and handling charges for orders over $50.00. Postage and handling rates are subject to change. UPS Delivery: We ship UPS whenever possible. Delivery guaranteed. Provide your street address as UPS does not deliver to P.O. Boxes. UPS to Canada requires a $50.00 minimum order. Allow 4-6 weeks for delivery. Orders outside the U.S.A. and Canada: Airmail—add retail price of book; add $5.00 for each non-book item (tapes, etc.); add $1.00 per item for surface mail.

FOR GROUP STUDY AND PURCHASE

Because there is a great deal of interest in group discussion and study of the subject matter of this book, we feel that we should encourage the adoption and use of this particular book by such groups by offering a special quantity" price to group leaders or agents."

Our Special Quantity Price for a minimum order of five copies of *Shamanism and the Esoteric Tradition* is $38.85 cash-with-order. This price includes postage and handling within the United States. Minnesota residents must add 6.5% sales tax. For additional quantities, please order in multiples of five. For Canadian and foreign orders, add postage and handling charges as above. Credit card (VISA, Master Card, American Express) orders are accepted. Charge card orders only may be phoned free ($15.00 minimum order) within the U.S.A. or Canada by dialing 1-800-THE-MOON. Customer service calls dial 1-612-291-1970. Mail orders to:

LLEWELLYN PUBLICATIONS
P.O. Box 64383, Dept. 325, St. Paul, MN 55164-383, U.S.A.

Prices subject to change without notice.

BIRTH OF A MODERN SHAMAN
A Documented Journey & Guide to Personal Transformation
by Cynthia Bend and Tayja Wiger

This is the amazing true story of Tayja Wiger. As a child she had been beaten and sexually abused. As an adult she was beaten and became a prostitute. To further her difficulties she was a member of a minority, a Native American Sioux, and was also legally blind.

Tayja's courage and will determined that she needed to make changes in her life. This book follows her physical and emotional healing through the use of Trans-actional Analysis and Re-Birthing, culminating in the healing of her blindness by the Spiritualistic Minister Marilyn Rossner, through the laying on of hands.

Astrology and graphology are used to show the changes in Tayja as her multiple personalities, another problem from which she suffered, were finally integrated into one. Tayja has become both a shaman and a healer

In *Birth of a Modem Shaman* there are powerful skills anyone can develop by becoming a shaman, the least of which is becoming balanced, at peace with the world around you, productive and happy. By using the techniques in this book, you will move toward a magickal understanding of the universe that can help you achieve whatever you desire, and can help you to become a modern shaman.

87542-034-6, 272 pgs., 6 x 9, illus., photos, softcover $9.95

GODWIN'S CABALISTIC ENCYCLOPEDIA
A Complete Guide to Cabalistic Magick
by David Godwin

This is the most complete correlation of Hebrew and English ideas ever offered. It is a dictionary of Cabalism arranged, with definitions, alphabetically in Hebrew and numerically. With this book, the practicing Cabalist or student no longer needs access to a large number of books on mysticism, magic and the occult in order to trace down the basic meanings, Hebrew spellings, and enumerations of the hundreds of terms, words, and names that are included in this book.

This book includes: all of the two-letter root words found in Biblical Hebrew, the many names of God, the Planets, the Astrological Signs, Numerous Angels, the Shem ha-Mephorash, the Spirits of the *Goetia*, the correspondences of the 32 Paths, a comparison of the Tarot and the Cabala, a guide to Hebrew Pronuncia-tion, and a complete edition of Aleister Crowley's valuable book *Sepher Sephiroth.*

Here is a book that is a must for the shelf of all Magicians, Cabalists, Astrologers, Tarot students, Thelemites, and those with any interest at all in the spiritual aspects of our universe.

0-87542-292-6, 528 pgs., 6 x 9, softcover $15.00

THE GOLDEN DAWN
The Original Account of the Teachings, Rites & Ceremonies of the Hermetic Order
As revealed by Israel Regardie

Complete in one volume with further revision, expansion, and additional notes by Regardie, Cris Monnastre, and others. Expanded with an index of more than 100 pages!

Originally published in four bulky volumes of some 1,200 pages, this 6th Revised and Enlarged Edition has been entirely reset in modern, less space-consuming type, in half the pages (while retaining the original pagination in marginal notation for reference) for greater ease and use.

Corrections of typographical errors perpetuated in the original and subsequent editions have been made, with further revision and additional text and notes by noted scholars and by actual practitioners of the Golden Dawn system of Magick, with an Introduction by the only student ever accepted for personal training by Regardie.

Also included are Initiation Ceremonies, important rituals for consecration and invocation, methods of meditation and magical working based on the Enochian Tablets, studies in the Tarot, and the system of Qabalistic Correspondences that unite the World's religions and magical traditions into a comprehensive and practical whole.

This volume is designed as a study and practice curriculum suited to both group and private practice. Meditation upon, and following with the Active Imagination, the Initiation Ceremonies are fully experiential without need of participation in group or lodge. A very complete reference encyclopedia of Western Magick.

0-87542-663-8, 840 pgs., 6 x 9, illus., softcover $19.95

MAGICAL DANCE
Your Body as an Instrument of Power
by Ted Andrews

Choreograph your own evolution through one of the most powerful forms of magickal ritual: Dance. When you let your inner spirit express itself through movement, you can fire your vitality, revive depleted energies, awaken individual creativity and transcend your usual perceptions.

Directed physical movement creates electrical changes in the body that create shifts in consciousness. It links the hemispheres of the brain, joining the rational and the intuitive to create balance, healing, strength and psychic energy.

This book describes and illustrates over 20 dance and other magickal movements and postures. Learn to shapeshift through dance, dance your prayers into manifestation, align with the planets through movement, activate and raise the kundalini, create group harmony and power, and much more. Anyone who can move any part of the body can perform magical movement. No formal dance training is required.

0-87542-004-4, 224 pgs., 6 x 9, illus., photos, softcover $9.95

MAGICIAN'S COMPANION
A Practical and Encyclopedic Guide to Magical and Religious Symbolism
by Bill Whitcomb

The Magician's Companion is a "desk reference" overflowing with a wide range of occult and esoteric materials absolutely indispensable to anyone engaged in the magickal arts!

The magical knowledge of our ancestors comprises an intricate and elegant technology of the mind and imagination. This book attempts to make the ancient systems accessible, understandable and useful to modern magicians by categorizing and cross-referencing the major magical symbol-systems (i.e., world views on inner and outer levels). Students of religion, mysticism, mythology, symbolic art, literature, and even cryptography will find this work of value.

This comprehensive book discusses and compares over 35 magical models (e.g., the Trinities, the Taoist Psychic Centers, Enochian magic, the qabala, the Worlds of the Hopi Indians). Also included are discussions of the theory and practice of magic and ritual; sections on alchemy, magical alphabets, talismans, sigils, magical herbs and plants; suggested programs of study; an extensive glossary and bibliography; and much more.

0-87542-868-1, 522 pgs., 7 x 10, illus., softcover $19.95

MODERN MAGICK
Eleven Lessons in the High Magickal Arts
by Donald Michael Kraig

Modern Magick is the most comprehensive step-by-step introduction to the art of ceremonial magic ever offered. The eleven lessons in this book will guide you from the easiest of rituals and the construction of your magickal tools through the highest forms of magick: designing your own rituals and doing pathworking. Along the way you will learn the secrets of the Kabbalah in a clear and easy-to-understand manner. You will also discover the true secrets of invocation (channeling) and evocation, and the missing information that will finally make the ancient grimoires, such as the "Keys of Solomon," not only comprehensible, but usable.

Modern Magick also covers such topics as the Tarot, Wicca, Words of Power, how to meditate, how to astral travel, the secrets of sex magick, creative visualization and much more. Each chapter has a bibliography, and at the end of the book there is an annotated bibliography as well as a glossary which explains the meanings of the unusual and foreign words. Each chapter also features self-tests so you can judge your own success at mastering the information.

Modern Magick is designed so anyone can use it, and it is the perfect guidebook for students and classes. It will also help to round out the knowledge of long-time practitioners of the magickal arts. As a result, it has become one of the most popular instruction books on magick of all time.

0-87542-324-8, 592 pgs., 6 x 9, illus., index, softcover $14.95

RITUAL MAGIC
What It Is & How To Do It
by Donald Tyson

For thousands of years men and women have practiced it despite the severe repression of sovereigns and priests. Now, *Ritual Magic* takes you into the heart of that entrancing, astonishing and at times mystifying secret garden of *magic*.

What is this ancient power? Where does it come from? How does it work? Is it mere myth and delusion, or can it truly move mountains and make the dead speak. . . bring rains from a clear sky and calm the seas. . . turn the outcome of great battles and call down the Moon from Heaven? Which part of the claims made for magic are true in the most literal sense, and which are poetic exaggerations that must be interpreted symbolically? How can magic be used to improve *your* life?

This book answers these and many other questions in a clear and direct manner. Its purpose is to separate the wheat from the chaff and make sense of the nonsense. It explains what the occult revival is all about, reveals the foundations of practical ritual magic, showing how modern occultism grew from a single root into a number of clearly defined esoteric schools and pagan sects.

0-87542-835-5, 288 pgs., 6 x 9, illus., index, softcover $12.95

SACRED SITES
A Guidebook to Sacred Centers & Mysterious Places in the United States
edited by Frank Joseph

Unknown to most Americans, our country has its own prehistoric pyramids—one larger at its base than its Egyptian counterpart! We have full-scale replicas of Stonehenge and the Parthenon, not in ruins, but as they appeared when new. Now, with *Sacred Sites*, you don't need to travel overseas, and to only the most famous sites, for a personal mystical experience at a spiritually charged spot of deep antiquity.

The United States is abundant with natural and man-made locations of unique and profound spiritual powers. *Sacred Sites* acquaints readers with more than 70 of them, provides their physical descriptions and suggests simple rituals for tapping into their special energies. Few persons who seek out the places described in *Sacred Sites* will fail to be impressed by their mystery and beauty.

The 27 contributors in this volume are intimately familiar with the locations about which they write. They tell you how to reach each site and how to fine-tune your innate sensitivities to their ancient voices and lingering energies. Contains 16 pages of color photographs!

0-87542-348-5, 424 pgs., 6 x 9, photos, softcover $16.95

IN THE SHADOW OF THE SHAMAN
Connecting with Self, Nature & Spirit
by Amber Wolfe

Presented in what the author calls a "cookbook shamanism" style, this book shares recipes, ingredients, and methods of preparation for experiencing some very ancient wisdoms: wisdoms of Native American and Wiccan traditions, as well as contributions from other philosophies of Nature as they are used in the shamanic way. Wheels, the circle, totems, shields, directions, divinations, spells, care of sacred tools and meditations are all discussed. Wolfe encourages us to feel confident and free to use her methods to cook up something new, completely on our own. This blending of ancient formulas and personal methods represents what Ms. Wolfe calls Aquarian Shamanism.

In the Shadow of the Shaman is designed to communicate in the most practical, direct ways possible, so that the wisdom and the energy may be shared for the benefits of all. Whatever your system or tradition, you will find this to be a valuable book, a resource, a friend, a gentle guide and support on your journey. Dancing in the shadow of the shaman, you will find new dimensions of Spirit.

0-87542-888-6, 384 pgs., 6 x 9, illus., softcover   **$12.95**

THE TRUTH ABOUT SHAMANISM
by Amber Wolfe

A primer on the basic ideas and techniques of shamanism, which is increasingly popular due to its deep spirituality, reverence for all life, and ability to provide answers for the world's troubles.

0-87542-889-4, 32 pgs., 5 1/2 x 8 1/2   **$2.00**

SIMPLE NATAL CHART

Your chart calculated by computer in the Tropical/Placidus House system or the House system of your choice. It has all of the trimmings, including aspects, midpoints, Chiron and a glossary of symbols, plus a free booklet!

APS03-119   **$5.00**